Mark Steensland

The Pocket Essential

MICHAEL MANN

First published in Great Britain 2002 by Pocket Essentials, 18 Coleswood Road,
Harpenden, Herts, AL5 1EQ

Distributed in the USA by Trafalgar Square Publishing, PO Box 257, Howe Hill
Road, North Pomfret, Vermont 05053

Copyright © Mark Steensland 2002
Series Editor: Steve Holland

A CIP catalogue record for this book is available from the British Library.

ISBN 1-903047-84-6

2 4 6 8 10 9 7 5 3 1

Book typeset by Pdunk
Printed and bound by Cox & Wyman

For K.

Acknowledgements

The author wishes to acknowledge the following, without whom this book would not have been possible: Michael Mann, Rick Shaffer, Paul Duncan, Ion Mills, Steve Holland, Frank Tomasulo, Victor Comerchero, Jonathan Ridenour, Eric Noak, Sean Leahy, Kristine Arnold, Sophie, Ben and, of course, the last who shall be first, J C.

CONTENTS

1. The World According To Michael Mann 7
In which the greatest crime is betrayal of self.

2. In The Beginning 13
From "The Patch" to London, Insurrection (1968), Jaunpuri (1970) and the Jury Prize at Cannes, 17 Days Down The Line (1972), Starsky & Hutch (1975), Police Story (1977), Vega$ (1978) and The Jericho Mile (1979)

3. Violent Streets 20
Thief (1981)

4. What Is This Place? 27
The Keep (1983)

5. Return To TV-Land 36
Miami Vice (1984) and Crime Story (1986)

6. Just You And Me Now, Sport 47
Manhunter (1986)

7. I Will Return 56
The Last Of The Mohicans (1992)

8. L.A. Crime Sagas 64
L.A. Takedown (1989) and Heat (1995)

9. Oscar Calling 78
The Insider (1999)

10. Into The Future Through The Past 86
Ali (2001)

11. After Effects 91
Complete Filmography, Projects Not Realized, Websites

1. The World According To Michael Mann

No doubt about it, Michael Mann is a maverick. Born in America and educated in Europe, his unique films combine these sensibilities in the most arresting and thought-provoking fashion. He is an existential action director, an A-list Hollywood 'name' who nonetheless makes what can best be called foreign films. For despite their orientation towards action couched in an MTV style, they are concerned with intellectual, moral and spiritual issues of life-altering magnitude. His films may be difficult, but they are never confusing. Like lasers, they are complex machines, wonderful to behold and filled with multi-layered interiors that reveal themselves to the wise viewer. He is a stylist in the best sense of the word, an artist and craftsman who uses every element at his disposal, not for its own sake, but only in order to communicate his message more effectively. If Hollywood knew how deep his movies really are, they would never give him another job. As it stands, he hardly allows himself the opportunity to work, choosing only to make films he truly believes in. As a result, he has directed just two films for television and seven theatrical features – including *Thief*, *Manhunter* and *The Insider* – since 1979. That his impact is so far-reaching with so small an output is perhaps the greatest testimony to his potency as a filmmaker.

So what makes a Michael Mann film? First and foremost, they are emotionally felt dramas. For although there are flashes of cynical humor, there isn't much to laugh at in Mann's filmic world, proof perhaps of the aphorism, "Life is a comedy for those who think; a tragedy for those who feel." And Mann's protagonists, who are exclusively male, definitely feel more than they think. This is, in fact, the primary source of their conflict: what they feel is in direct opposition to what they think. Will Graham in *Manhunter* knows he shouldn't go back to work, but he feels that he must. What's more, Graham pursues The Tooth Fairy not by deducing his way to a solution, but by feeling his way. He's in danger because he knows he must become the killer in order to catch him. Similarly, Jeffrey Wigand in *The Insider* knows that he should simply be quiet, but he feels that he must bring the truth to light, even if it costs him everything. In short, Mann's men believe more than those around them. These men are more dedicated to what they do than anyone else. Their zeal is nothing short of religious. And although they may be alone at the end of their stories, their victories are never Phyrric but very real. They succeed as martyrs do. Their saint-hood is guaranteed. They are not destroyed because these men know they are alone and because of that, the worst crime in a Michael Mann film is not thievery or killing, but betrayal of self.

Starting with this kind of story, Mann then writes a screenplay stripped to the barest essentials. Even when the films themselves run longer than the typical multiplex fare, the scripts never stop to smell the roses. Instead, they rocket through to the moment of truth. His dialogue is like another language, not, however, in a kind of fake science-fiction fashion, but in a very hard-won realistic sense. The overwhelming feel-ing is that Mann hasn't made this stuff up. And he hasn't. The dialogue in *Thief* rings so true precisely because Mann employed so many real cops and robbers as technical advisors.

Armed with a realistic screenplay, Mann then sets about designing his films from the bottom up. Production design, costume design, art direction and set decoration are all brought into play in a way that underscores what's in the script. For *The Insider*, this attention to detail even influenced such things as wallpaper patterns, consciously chosen by Mann and his design department to reflect the interior state of the characters in particular scenes. Once these elements have been assem-bled, another layer of reality is added by employing real props. For *Thief*, this meant that while the interior of the jewelry broker's office in Los Angeles was a carefully designed set, a real vault door and a real magnesium burn bar were brought in so that James Caan and crew could really burn through the vault.

With all this in place, Mann then takes an almost documentary approach to shooting the individual scenes. As he did in his earliest days as a filmmaker, Mann operates his own camera much of the time, shooting coverage of his scenes as if they are real events happening in real time – as they often are. The result is more like a documentary than a typical fiction film and explains why he so often requires multiple edi-tors to cull through the millions of feet of film in search of those cap-tured moments of reality. Mann then adds sound and music in much the same way he employs production design: to reflect the emotional interiors of the particular scenes. The end result is an ultra-realistic record of pretend people doing real things all in the service of the truth he's telling.

It's an approach that has been evident from the beginning of his career. His first feature as a director, *The Jericho Mile*, is astonishing not only for its ability to capture the reality of life inside a maximum security penitentiary while remaining sanitized enough for network broadcast, but also because it succeeds as drama so moving one could easily mistake it for having been based on a true story. What ultimately saves it from the common small-screen pitfall of sentimentality, however, is the stylized realism that is Mann's trademark. No wonder he won an Emmy for his script and a special Director's Guild Of America award for his direction.

With his next film, *Thief*, his first theatrical feature, Mann proved that more money and more time can indeed make a better film. Like Frank, the title character, Mann employed the better tools at his disposal to cut through the vault wall of what was passing for movies in America at the time of its release. Many critics (including Roger Ebert, who put it on his top ten films of the year list) recognized it instantly as something completely new and completely unique. So different was it though from *Chariots Of Fire*, *On Golden Pond* and *Arthur* that it was virtually ignored by film-goers at the time. It has since been marked as a watershed, enjoying a prominent position in a recent "Neo-noir" film retrospective in New York.

Undaunted by the vagaries of such things as box office and reviews, however, Mann, like his protagonists, refused to respond to anything but himself and for his next film, he turned 180 degrees from the streets of Chicago to Romania, circa 1941. Blasted by critics and still despised today by many, *The Keep* is nonetheless a Michael Mann film in its every frame. Presented as a fairy tale and executed in a style that consciously imitates German Expressionism, *The Keep* takes Mann's obsession with protagonists engaging in dangerous deals into the supernatural realm. Curiously, the result confused critics and failed to perform at the box office.

Following the disappointments of *The Keep*, Mann returned to television to executive-produce an episodic show called *Miami Vice*. And while many mistakenly believe Mann created the show, he in fact only served as its executive producer. The "created by" credit belongs to former *Hill Street Blues* producer and writer Anthony Yerkovich. What Mann did was import to the small screen what he had learned on *Thief*. And it worked. *Miami Vice* became a monster – an Emmy Award-winning, culture-changing, career-launching monster. Viewed now, more than a decade since its fifth and final season, this almost seems impossible. Its style and substance was so influential that it has ultimately rendered itself an irrelevant relic, a decade-defining cliché. What is more apparent, however, is just how much Mann defined that style by imprinting his own sensibilities onto what could have been simply another failed *Hill Street Blues* knock-off. The cinematography, production design (particularly the costuming), editing, sound and music (especially the music) combine to form a deceptively pretty cocktail. Cleansed of real pungency by the requirements of television, audiences took to it in a way that they hadn't taken to *Thief*, which had been released only four years before. Apparently the rest of the world just had to catch up with Mann who was, like so many great artists, running way ahead of his time.

Buoyed by the remarkable success of *Miami Vice*, NBC wanted to have another Mann franchise on hand and *Crime Story* was rushed into place. Created by Chuck Adamson and Gustave Reininger, Mann again acted as executive producer, imprinting his style on someone else's material. Viewed back to back now, it's hard not to assess *Crime Story* as the more successful effort. That it lasted only two seasons is testimony more to its sharper edges than any lack in quality. So with *Miami Vice* still red-hot and *Crime Story* on its way, Mann finally returned to the big screen once again.

As he had done with both his previous theatrical films, Mann again adapted a novel. This time, the book was *Red Dragon*, by Thomas Harris. A former AP news reporter who had been stationed in the Middle East, Harris had turned to writing fiction full-time when his first novel, *Black Sunday*, a terrorist thriller, made it onto the best-seller lists and was turned into a high-profile Hollywood movie. *Red Dragon* is of course now known as the book that introduced Hannibal Lecter, but it was also unique in that its author had done extensive research with the then-emerging Behavioral Science Division of the FBI. It's hard to believe, but yes, serial killers were then a relatively new phenomenon. Because of this combination of intense realism and a central character that could have been conceived by Mann himself, it's easy to see why the book so appealed to him. Rendered in the same stylized realism as Frank's criminal activities in *Thief*, *Manhunter* is a veritable doppel-gänger of the earlier film. Unfortunately, producer Dino De Laurentiis thought audiences would be confused by the title, either associating it with Michael Cimino's bomb *Year Of The Dragon* or *Red Sonja*, his own attempt to create a Conan sub-franchise. Rather unwisely, he changed the title to *Manhunter* so that even fans of the book didn't know what it was. Like *Thief* all over again, the movie electrified critics but failed to find an audience. And like *Thief*, the movie has been recently reassessed, properly recognized now for its far-reaching influence.

Within two years, both *Miami Vice* and *Crime Story* were off the air and Mann was back at the starting line. In 1989, he dug out a script called *Heat*, penned before *The Keep*, and turned it into a quickie TV movie titled *L.A. Takedown*. Largely unremarkable, the film has a hurried air about it, due principally to the fact that Mann didn't have the proper resources to do his script justice.

Over the next three years, Mann remained in television working to bring *Drug Wars* to the small screen as an epic mini-series. The true story of DEA Agent Enrique 'Kiki' Camarena, *Drug Wars* earned Mann another Emmy and another shot at going back to the big screen. Tired of cops-and-robbers (I don't know why!), Mann surprised everyone by launching a remake of *The Last Of The Mohicans*. Again using a novel as his source material, Mann also based his new version on Philip Dunne's screenplay for the 1936 adaptation of the film. Casting Daniel Day-Lewis (at the time known only to art-house audiences as the guy from *My Left Foot*) opposite Madeline Stowe was a match made in Hollywood heaven. Their romance, set against a violent backdrop, all executed in the by now trademark Mann style was finally the mixture audiences had been looking for. The film was – and still is – Mann's most successful strictly in box office terms. Finally, he had proven himself a force to be reckoned with, a film-maker who not only scored with critics but with audiences as well. The Academy acknowledged his new status by awarding his film the Oscar for achievement in sound.

At last, Mann could leave TV behind forever. At last, he had earned the Golden Ticket and he decided to use it to remake *L.A. Takedown* in the right way. Changing the title back to the original *Heat*, Mann attracted both Robert De Niro and Al Pacino, putting them together on screen for the first time. The result was monumental, scoring worldwide with critics and audiences alike.

Again rolling up the cops-and-robbers backdrop, Mann returned to his documentary roots after a fashion for his next film. *The Insider*, based on the true story of tobacco company whistle-blower Jeffrey Wigand and his relationship with news giant *60 Minutes*, is Mann's best film yet, earning 7 Oscar nominations, including one for Mann as best director and one for best picture. When Russell Crowe lost in the Best Actor category to Kevin Spacey only to return the next year and win for *Gladiator*, word on the street was that his *Gladiator* statuette was really for *The Insider*.

Coming off such recognition, hopes for *Ali*, Mann's next film, run high. And in spite of concerns about Will Smith having the necessary dramatic depth to pull off such a difficult role, there can be little doubt that it will be a Michael Mann film through and through. The guy doesn't know how to do anything else.

2. In The Beginning

Born in Chicago on February 5, 1943, Mann grew up near "The Patch," one of the Windy City's roughest areas. How rough? Mann once estimated that only 13 out of the 365 students in his high school graduating class went on to college. He was one of them, choosing English Literature as his major at the University of Wisconsin in Madison. While at college, he saw G W Pabst's masterpiece of silent cinema, *The Joyless Street*, and caught the movie bug. Wanting to get into film-making as a full time career, Mann looked at American film schools but was disappointed by their vocational approach to the subject. So in 1965, Mann left America and went to Europe, entering the London International Film School. There, he did what he thought he should do: make student films, not a show reel – the kind of films he once described as "two-and-a-half minute, fully symbolic statements on the nature of reality that'll shame you 10 years later."

After earning his Master's Degree from L.I.F.S., Mann remained in London for six years, forming his own production company and mostly making commercials. But this wasn't his real passion and the money he earned was quickly applied to his own projects. Among them was *Insurrection*, a documentary about the student uprisings in Paris, France, in May 1968. His first break came when some of the footage he had shot for *Insurrection* was used in NBC's *First Tuesday* news program because NBC's own crew had been unable to get close to the radical leaders. Then, in 1970, Mann received worldwide attention when his short film, *Jaunpuri*, won the Jury Prize at Cannes. But his career was still going nowhere.

Missing life in the United States, Mann divorced his first wife, left behind what he called a "swinging London lifestyle" and returned home. With the Cannes prize and a substantial list of credits on his resume, he settled in Southern California and began shopping his first screenplay around, assuming that he would land a job directing within 30 days or so. No such luck. Instead, he directed *17 Days Down The Line*, a documentary for ABC that was, appropriately enough, about a road trip from Chicago to Los Angeles. But when his original thirty-day plan stretched out to nearly three years, Mann didn't know what to do.

Then he met Robert Lewin. A writer who had cut his teeth on *Rawhide* and *Hawaii Five-O*, Lewin taught Mann screenplay structure. When he became a story editor for *Starsky & Hutch*, he also gave Mann his first real writing job. And although somewhat at odds with his true desires as a film-maker, Mann saw television for what it was: something to get into, shoot and get out of fast.

After writing the first four episodes of *Starsky & Hutch*, Mann then wrote five episodes of Joseph Wambaugh's *Police Story*, what he once called "the Rolls-Royce of TV shows." Then, at the suggestion of Fred Silverman, he created the hit series *Vega$*, featuring Robert Urich as Dan Tanna, the Las Vegas detective with the drive-in house. Originally conceived with a much rougher center – Mann had Kerouac in mind when he wrote the script – the show ended up in the hands of a producer who was into white patent leather and became something Mann no longer recognized. He quickly left the show and all but disowns it today. Nonetheless, *Vega$* was a hit and he managed to parlay the show's success into some directing assignments, including episodes of *Police Woman*, the Angie Dickinson TV series, and an uncredited rewrite of *Straight Time*, which starred Dustin Hoffman.

But Mann wanted to make features and finally, like so many of his protagonists in his later films, he was ready to do anything for what he believed in and he issued an ultimatum to ABC: "Let me direct or I'll quit writing." The tactic worked and reluctant executives allowed him to peruse their library of unproduced scripts. He quickly found what he was looking for. It was called *The Jericho Mile*.

The Jericho Mile (1979)

Directed by Michael Mann. Written by Michael Mann and Patrick J Nolan, from a story by Patrick J Nolan.

The Cast: Peter Strauss (Rain Murphy), Richard Lawson (R C Stiles), Brian Dennehy (Dr D), Geoffrey Lewis (Dr Bill Janowski), Billy Green Bush (Warden Earl Gulliver), Ed Lauter (Jerry Beloit)

The Crew: Produced by Tim Zinnemann. Music by Jimmie Haskell. Photographed by Rexford Metz. Edited by Arthur Schmidt. Art Direction by Stephen Myles Berger. 95 minutes.

The Coverage: Inside Folsom State Penitentiary, inmates Murphy and Stiles do their time by running. When prison officials take an interest in Murphy and have him clocked, they discover that he is running close to a four-minute mile and they quickly arrange to have a track coach brought in from a nearby university to find out what he's really made of. Meanwhile, Stiles receives a letter from his wife containing a picture of his new baby, and he resolves to do whatever it takes to see them sooner than their next scheduled visit, even if it means crossing a political line. For Stiles, who is Black, that means making a deal with Dr D, the leader of the White Power Party. This upsets his fellow Blacks, but it's too late. With the deal done, Stiles heads to his conjugal visit while Murphy meets the track coach and runners on the yard. Murphy impresses everyone by setting a time only four seconds off the second fastest runner in the United States. The Warden and the Coach want Murphy to begin training for the Olympic trials right away, but Murphy surprises them by saying he can't do it. Meanwhile, in the visiting area, Stiles looks for his wife, but is instead met by a woman hired by Dr D to mule drugs into the prison. Stiles refuses to go along with the scam and suspicious guards capture the woman and confiscate the drugs and money. When Murphy hears what happened, he pledges to help Stiles get off the mainline and into isolation where he'll be safe. But Dr D's men kill Stiles before Murphy can help him. Seeking his own form of revenge, Murphy tells the prison officials he'll run as long as they let him into the metal shop alone for half-an-hour right then. There, Murphy tears the place apart until he finds Dr D's stash of cash. He takes it to the yard and burns it all in front of everyone. Furious, Dr D tells Murphy he's a dead man. Hopes for Murphy soar until the Warden is told that he can't let him out of the prison to run in a qualifying race. Unwilling to let this unique opportunity go, the Warden decides to get the inmates to help him build an official track inside the prison so they can run the race right there. But Dr D and his crew form a picket line and prevent the other inmates from helping to build the track. Meanwhile, the Black Power leaders confront Dr D about his role in Stiles' death. Dr D tells them it was Murphy who sent Stiles up. Enraged, the leader of the Black Power group corners Murphy and beats him to a pulp. But when Murphy tells him the truth – that Stiles was his brother – the Blacks decide to help Murphy and enlist the aid of the Latinos to cross Dr D's picket line. A riot erupts, the line is crossed and the once-divided prison population now works together to build the track as fast as they can. Cheered on by the whole prison, Murphy runs the race and wins. With a qualifying time in place, Murphy will be able to go to the Olympic trials in Los Angeles. But the O.A.U. board explains that because Murphy is an inmate – a convicted murderer – they cannot allow him to run in their race. The dream shattered, everyone returns to where they were at the beginning. Instead of working together as they had, the racial factions within the prison have split again. When Murphy hears the results of the trials in Los Angeles, he heads to the track and runs a race alone, beating the winning time.

Research: Mann's working method is always to begin with a period of thorough background research. Even with this, his first film, he didn't know any other way to work. And it shows. When he hunted down everything he could about prison subcultures, one of the elements he discovered was the overwhelming pride in the sports sections of the prison newspapers. He rightfully assumed that no one dared criticize anyone else because they would earn a beating in the process. And he promptly worked this into the script as an effective method not only for introducing his main character, but also the three power groups – the Blacks, the Latinos and the Whites – creating what he called "social Technicolor." He also learned a lot about the sort of coded language employed in prison and the different meanings that are communicated by the specific cadences and forms contained in those speech patterns. Lack of contractions, for instance, equals greater importance so that

"I'll tell you what's up" has less import than "I will tell you what is up." The result is a level of authenticity unmatched in most TV movies.

Story: Michael Mann's stories are always the same on a philosophical level. They always concern a man caught in a deal that is dangerous to take. These deals are essentially what existential philosopher Karl Barth called "boundary situations," defining moments entered with two choices: erect more smoke and mirrors to occlude yourself further from the truth or pull down those mirrors and become more transparent, more true, more real. And although the smoke and mirrors take many forms in a Michael Mann film – whether it be material goods (like money) or external attachments (like relationships) – Mann's protagonists always choose to become more real, to get out of their deal with the devil and take a step towards heaven. *The Jericho Mile* is no exception. Deals fill the air inside Folsom prison – everyone's makin' 'em: Stiles with Dr D, the Latinos with the Blacks, Murphy and the Coach – everyone has entangled themselves with someone. In Mann's world, such entanglements are dangerous because they involve other people. And when you get involved with other people, you lose control. The only way to maintain control is to cut off these entanglements, as Murphy does. Thus Murphy becomes the first shining example of the Mann Man.

The Mann Man: Every protagonist in a Michael Mann film has three common characteristics. First, they are alone in their dedication to what they do. Second, they enter a deal they believe will give them something they lack. Third, they ultimately realize the deal is dangerous because it is beyond their control, and that the only thing within their control is their inner self. Murphy could hardly fit the definition more perfectly. He begins the story dedicated to one thing: running. In fact, Murphy doesn't do anything but run. This attitude has by necessity been born out of his situation. If he failed to acknowledge the truth of where he is, he would come apart at the seams, like those around him. When asked by the prison shrink if his running takes him somewhere else, Murphy tells him clearly that it does not. "I am here," he says, "I'm not anywhere else." This sounds perilously similar to mid-70s "Be Here Now" kind of self-help, but that doesn't take away from the clearly spiritual nature of his choice. Nonetheless, because of his attachment to Stiles, he allows himself to form his own attachments to the Warden, the Coach and the dream of achieving something beyond the walls that contain him. In the end, of course, he learns the truth of what he knew all along: that he cannot have those attachments. But this is not as depressing as it sounds. It is, rather, uplifting because Murphy has remained true to himself. Rather than lie to the O.A.U. authorities just to get a chance at running in the Olympic trials, Murphy tells the truth: that he would kill his father again. And although he loses out on the opportunity to achieve the larger dream, he also knows that to have betrayed himself simply to achieve that dream would have rendered it meaningless. Thus, when he runs the race at the end of the movie against the time that he knows won the Olympic trials, he appropriately runs alone. And when he wins, his victory is more real and true than anything else he has achieved to that point. That he hurls his watch at the walls of the prison tells us, quite literally, that he has defeated time.

Design: While later films would find Mann going to great lengths in terms of design, *The Jericho Mile* is unique because the lack of design actually creates a stronger effect. In other words, the fact that Mann was allowed to shoot inside the walls at Folsom necessitated an approach that lends greater realism to the end product. Nothing we see on screen is fake. Nothing has been built. Those aren't extras in the background – they're real prisoners! Even the lighting appears to be coming mostly from existing practical sources. This is exactly the way Mann would have been required to shoot the movie if he had been shooting a documentary inside the prison walls. And ultimately, all this reality only makes the story itself seem more real.

Shooting And Cutting: From the opening, Mann's mastery of cinematic techniques is explosively evident. The pre-credits sequence – a montage in which Murphy's running, scenes depicting the political intrigues of the various racial factions within the prison and abstract shots of a giant mural are all intercut – is a tour de force of visual storytelling. Mann also masterfully uses editing to underscore certain facets of the story. So that while many of the scenes employ very little editing, the running sequences, by contrast, are built out of numerous shots. Different angles, different lens lengths and different camera speeds are all combined to put the viewer directly into the race. But this approach also has the effect of making the running stand out more from the other scenes in the film – and rightfully so, for it is his running which enables Murphy to lift his head above the other, more pedestrian activities within the prison.

Music: For Mann, one of the most powerful tools at his disposal is music. And as with every other option, he is not influenced by personal taste, but is instead obsessed with employing the most effective devices to enhance the meaning of the story he's telling. *The Jericho Mile* is a prime example of this approach. From its opening drum line, the main theme is a piece of music we instantly recognize as 'Sympathy For The Devil' by the Rolling Stones. And what better music could he use to establish his main character than a song about having sympathy for someone the world perceives as evil? Murphy (and his fellow prisoners) are all devils and Mann is telling us, solely through his use of music, that this is going to be a story about having sympathy for men such as these. What makes this musical introduction especially remarkable is the fact that there are no words and yet anyone even lightly familiar with the tune can tell you what it is and, therefore, what it's about. So striking, in fact, was the opening sequence that it has since been pointed to as a direct influence on the then-emerging form of the music video. An irony given Mann's later association with *Miami Vice*, a show sometimes referred to as "MTV cops."

The Final Word: This is a movie that both defines Mann's style and his approach to the craft of film-making. Given the career of films that follows, *The Jericho Mile* is also a unique opportunity to see nearly all of Mann's obsessions on display for the first time. Even though made for television, it has been called "a prison film unlike any other" by *Rolling Stone* and ranks as one of the best movies in Mann's oeuvre. Winning both an Emmy Award for writing and a special Director's Guild of America Award for directing, *The Jericho Mile* was an auspicious beginning for the 36-year-old filmmaker. And while sadly out of print on home video, this is definitely one to hunt down. Position on the Mann Top Ten List: #6.

NB: *The Jericho Mile* is co-writer Patrick J. Nolan's only screen credit. While all the extras in the film are real prisoners, Mann even allowed some of them to play minor speaking roles. While shooting inside Folsom, thirteen stabbings occurred and one inmate was killed.

3. Violent Streets

Within three days of *The Jericho Mile*'s debut on ABC, Mann was offered 22 feature films. In a bold move, he turned every one of them down and went to United Artists to ask for an $8 million budget and carte blanche to direct a screenplay he had written based on *The Home Invaders*, a book by a real-life thief named Frank Hohimer. Subtitled *Confessions Of A Cat Burglar*, the book is more a collection of remembered facts rather than any kind of concrete story. As such, however, Mann had ideal source material: voluminous research laid out in anecdotal form, filled with true stories and real language from which he could build his own tale. UA agreed and the result was *Thief*, a blistering assault on the senses that remains undiluted by time.

Thief (1981)

Directed by Michael Mann. Screenstory and Screenplay by Michael Mann, based on *The Home Invaders* by Frank Hohimer.

The Cast: James Caan (Frank), Tuesday Weld (Jessie), Willie Nelson (Okla), James Belushi (Barry), Robert Prosky (Leo), Tom Signorelli (Attaglia), Dennis Farina (Carl), John Santucci (Urizzi), Chuck Adamson (Ancell), William Petersen (Bartender)

The Crew: Produced by Jerry Bruckheimer and Ronnie Caan. Music by Tangerine Dream and Craig Safan. Photographed by Donald Thorin. Edited by Dov Hoenig. Production Designed by Mel Bourne. Technical Consultants Chuck Adamson and John Santucci. 122 minutes. Aka *Violent Streets*.

The Coverage: Frank and his crack team of thieves break into a vault and steal boxes of unmounted diamonds. The next day, Frank meets Joe Gags, his fence, in a diner. Gags tells Frank some people want to meet him. Frank refuses, saying he has no interest, then asks the cashier, Jessie, out to dinner. Back at his day job as a used-car salesman, Frank receives a letter from David "Okla" Bertineau, his former cell-mate at Joliet State Penitentiary. In his letter, Okla says he needs to see him right away. Frank takes an odd collage of images out of his wallet and stares at it for a long moment. At another one of his businesses, the

Green Mill Bar And Lounge, Frank receives a call from Barry, his partner in crime. Barry tells him that he went to see Gags, but Gags had been killed. Barry promises to find out what happened and Frank rushes to meet him. Barry discovers that Gags had crossed another criminal, named Attaglia, and that's why he was killed. However, the money that Gags had with him when he was killed was Frank's money. Together, he and Barry visit L & A Plating Company, where Attaglia works. Inside, Frank tells Attaglia he wants his money. At first, Attaglia feigns ignorance, but when Frank pulls a gun and tells him he is the last person in the world to mess with, Attaglia promises to get Frank his money. At Joliet, Okla tells Frank that he has a heart condition and he won't survive past his sentence. He wants Frank to get him out. Frank promises to help him. That night, Frank goes to pick up his money and meets Leo, Attaglia's boss. Leo, it turns out, was the guy Gags had told Frank about. Under police surveillance, Leo tells Frank he wants to hire him as a contract thief. Frank doesn't believe in long-term arrangements. Leo says Frank can just give it a try and Frank promises to think about it. At dinner with Jessie that night, Frank shows her his collage and explains that it represents the life he wants – a house, a wife, kids – and he wants her to be part of it. She refuses at first, but Frank insists, promising that he has a way to make it happen very fast. She relents. Leo, Frank and Barry visit Los Angeles, where Frank's first big score for Leo will take place. Frank then visits Sam, a specialist, to enlist his aid in figuring out how to get into the vault. At court, Frank buys off a corrupt judge to get Okla out of prison. Frank tells Barry that this job is going to be his last. Starting their new life, Frank and Jessie try to adopt a child but their application is refused when Frank's criminal past is revealed. Frank is pulled over by the police and Urizzi, a corrupt cop, tells Frank that he gets a piece of his action with Leo. Frank feigns ignorance. Urizzi doesn't understand. Frank now finds his house is bugged. He visits Leo and complains that as soon as he got in with him, everyone knew his business. Leo promises to take care of it all – including the problem Frank has with adoption. He will do this by buying him a black-market baby. Frank is happy again. He calls Jessie to tell her the good news and instead finds out that Okla is in the hospital. They go to see him, but it's too late – Okla dies after thanking Frank for getting him out. Frank and Jessie pick up their new baby and decide to name him David, after Okla. Sam succeeds in making a tool to cut through the vault. They are set. Then Urizzi and his buddies arrest Frank and take him to the police station where they beat him up and explain that they will get what they want or they will take him down. Frank refuses to give in, telling them they should work for a living. They let Frank go. Frank loses the police surveillance team by putting their bug on a bus to Des Moines, then he, Barry and the crew head to Los Angeles where they successfully steal millions of dollars in diamonds. After vacationing a few days, Frank returns to Chicago and visits Leo to pick up his money. He is disappointed to find only a fraction of what he was supposed to get. Leo explains that he invested the rest of Frank's money in shopping centers. Frank is very upset. He tells Leo that he wants his money in 24 hours or he will kill them all. At the used car, Frank sees Leo's men kill Barry. They take Frank to a warehouse where Leo tells him that he can never stop working for him. He owns everything that Frank is. They let him go. Frank returns home, wakes Jessie up and tells her to get out. Frank then blows up his house, his bar and his car lot and goes to Leo's house. In a final shoot-out, Frank kills Leo and his men, then wanders into the night alone.

Research: Starting again with careful pre-production research, Mann used his relationships with members of the Chicago Police Department to gain access to real thieves. One inspiration was John Bardolino, a Chicago thief who stole over $10 million in jewels, cash, rare coins and precious metals over the course of his career. These real-life cops and criminals were brought together under Mann's guidance to collaborate on what is probably one of the greatest examples of an American crime film. Without the epic sentimentality of Coppola's *Godfather* trilogy and without the sort of macho posing and play-acting that infect so much of the genre thanks to Quentin Tarantino and his imitators, *Thief* remains timeless and relevant precisely because of its intense realism. Much of this was on paper in the form of the screenplay Mann had written. And although credited in part to Hohimer's book, Mann also put in lots of other tidbits he found in his research. For instance, the story that Frank tells Jessie – about his encounter with the brutal prison crew who wanted to rape him – was true, heard first-hand from a prisoner Mann had talked to. The character of Sam, the scrap-yard owner who builds Frank the 'burning bar' tool for the LA score, was based on the grandfather of one of Mann's childhood friends. Many of the actors in the film are real cops and crooks. Even the tools and guns used in the film were tools and guns that had been used on real robberies by the real thieves who were serving as Mann's technical advisors. And instead of rehearsing his lead actor, Mann required James Caan to spend four weeks prior to the start of principal photography hanging out with both the cops and the crooks. A tactic he's used ever since, this creates what Mann calls an "attitudinal" factor in performances. So effective was this approach, in fact, that James Caan has pointed to *Thief* as his greatest screen performance ever.

Story: With *Thief*, Mann takes the notion of 'the deal' as existential boundary situation back to its roots. With Leo as Mephistopheles to Frank's Faust, the whole movie is about a Faustian bargain. That Leo is the devil is made clear from his first appearance in which he comes to Frank as an angel of light: a straightforward, generous gentleman. He is, in effect, the absent father returned, telling Frank such things as "I'd be your father" and "I'm gonna give you everything you need, kid." He even "fathers" the child Frank can't have with Jessie. Frank, on the other hand, believes that he doesn't have what he needs to make his life complete. He thinks he wants to be distracted by the mirrors of having a beautiful wife, a big house, lots of money, nice clothes, nice cars, a perfect kid. And he makes his deal with Leo in order to get those things. At last, of course, Frank sees that he really has sold his soul and in order to get it back, he must end his deal with Leo and take control of his life again. To do this, he must cut off his connection with everything that is outside of him. Mann tells us this is an explosive process in a brilliant montage of jump-cutting and slow motion in which Frank literally blows up everything he owns, ending at last with 'Rocket Motors' going up in smoke. Oh yeah: this guy is definitely a Mann Man.

The Mann Man: One could easily mistake Frank and Murphy for brothers. And in a sense they are. They both learned their philosophies in prison. They are both dedicated to what they do. They both seek out attachments as a way of getting something they think they lack. And they both have difficult epiphanies. What's interesting, then, is the way that Mann expands and refracts the things we first saw in Murphy in the character of Frank. Where Murphy's dream is represented by his running, Frank's dream is made explicit in the form of the collage he carries in his wallet. But this collage can never be achieved because it is not true to Frank's inner self. This is made literal by the fact that the collage has been constructed from other people's ideas: the pictures representing what he wants have been cut from newspapers and magazines. This dream pushes Frank to seek out attachments. But he soon comes to understand, like Murphy, that these attachments are stifling rather than liberating. At last, Frank realizes he must destroy this collage in order to remain true to himself. As the film closes, Frank is back where he started. Unbelievably, this is not an unhappy ending. Had he stayed on with Leo just so that he could maintain his collage, Frank would have been far worse off. Who would want to see Leo do all the things he threatened to do with Frank and his family? That Mann manages to make this the really horrifying potential outcome is testimony to how strongly he communicates the truth of his philosophy. As a final statement about the nature of his sacrifice, the last shot of the film finds Frank on a sidewalk that forms, appropriately enough, a giant crucifix.

Design: Working with Mel Bourne, an Oscar-nominated art director who had graduated to full-fledged production designer on Woody Allen movies, Mann had the opportunity to carefully build Frank's environments to reflect his character. This is especially evident in the color schemes of the film. Green, for instance, becomes the color of danger and death. Most of the times Frank gets bad news, he is on the phone in his bar, The Green Mill, the windows behind him covered with green shades. Frank tells the adoption agency worker that he was state-raised, that he grew up in "eight-by-four green walls." The lamps in Leo's house all have green shades. When Barry is killed, he is wearing a green satin jacket. And at last, the final confrontation between Frank and Leo's men takes place on an expansive green lawn. By contrast, blue becomes Frank's color and represents the world he occupies. He often wears blue. He drives a blue car. Jessie wears a blue outfit when Frank asks her to dinner. Frank sits in front of a blue fence while he reads the letter from Okla. And, of course, Okla's outfit is standard-issue "prison blues." Grey becomes the color of the police, with most of them wearing grey coats and pants, as if Mann is telling us they are, quite literally, a combination of black and white – cops and crooks at the same time. Even the interior of the police department office where they take Frank for a beating is grey and green. Mann's conscious attention to design finds its way even into the structure of the film. As any screenwriting student can tell you, standard three-act structure dictates that the first "turning point" should occur one quarter of the way into a script, or on about page 30. In a sly comment on his awareness of this, the first turning point in *Thief* not only occurs exactly 30 minutes in but features Mighty Joe Young, a Blues band, singing a song that is appropriately called "Turning Point."

Shooting And Cutting: Mann's power as a visual stylist is evident from the very start, where ten minutes pass with hardly any dialogue. Rarely in the cinema – particularly in American cinema – has there been such a use of pure visuals. Nor is it because Mann is at a loss for words (just look at the huge dialogue scenes which follow), these characters aren't talking because they're criminals performing a jewel heist – they'd better not talk! The only words they exchange ("Are you clear?" "You're clear here." "Yeah. Come on.") are the only words these characters really would exchange. Frank and Barry don't even say "Good night" to each other as they get in their cars at the end of the job. Imagine the same scene remade by a lesser director and we'd no doubt have the criminals smart-mouthing to each other over the radio, slapping each other on the back after the job is complete, and driving away with tires squealing as they head off to party. Mann is not interested in such adolescent fantasies. He is interested in the truth and he will stop at nothing to take us there with him.

Music: As with *The Jericho Mile*, Mann again eschewed a traditional orchestral score, choosing instead to commission one written by German electronic band Tangerine Dream. He had wanted to use a Chicago-style Blues soundtrack, but like his first film, his choice ultimately had more to do with directly reflecting the story rather than personal taste. Thus the completely inorganic sounds of Tangerine Dream's score serve as a reflection of the tools of Frank's trade. As he uses modern technology to bypass alarm systems and break into vaults, so Tangerine Dream uses modern technology to reflect and underscore that sensibility. At the time, Tangerine Dream had only scored one other film, William Friedkin's disastrous remake of *Wages Of Fear*, *Sorcerer*. Following *Thief*, Tangerine Dream launched a lengthy second career as in-demand film composers.

The Final Word: With a potency far surpassing *The Jericho Mile*, *Thief* explodes onto the screen, grabs you by the throat and never lets you go. It is an assault on the senses at every level, a veritable pistol-whipping that leaves you devastated no matter how many times you've seen it before. When it opened on March 27, 1981, Sheila Benson of the *Los Angeles Times* called it "bravura film-making" and said that Mann had "declared war on the passive audience." Leonard Maltin called it a "stylishly photographed, arresting drama." David Ansen of *Newsweek* and Siskel & Ebert of *At The Movies* all gave it solid rave reviews – it even made Roger Ebert's Top Ten Films Of The Year list! Mann's obsessions, on display in seed form in *The Jericho Mile*, are here given full bloom by his access to greater resources. The end result is a movie that further defines Mann's style and approach to film-making and is, like *The Jericho Mile*, something so authentic that one could mistake it for having been based on a true story.

Unfortunately, it failed to find an audience in its initial theatrical run, earning only $4.3 million in the US. After the success of *Miami Vice*, however, and the film's re-issue in a special Director's Edition DVD, it has been reassessed as an overlooked masterpiece. If you've never seen a Michael Mann movie, this is the best place to start. Position on the Mann Top Ten List: #4.

NB: Frank Hohimer, author of *The Home Invaders*, was still in prison as the movie went into production. Dennis Farina, Robert Prosky, James Belushi and William Petersen all made their screen debuts in *Thief*. John Santucci, who plays Urizzi, was a real-life criminal and served as one of the movie's technical advisors. Censors demanded cuts to the safe-cracking scenes because they were too detailed. The last shot, in which the injured James Caan stands up into the frame, is an exact quote of a shot from the opening of another existential crime movie, John Boorman's *Point Blank*.

4. What Is This Place?

After *Thief*, the last thing Mann wanted to do was what he called another "street" picture. But in an environment that so favors pigeon-holing, that was what he was getting offered. In fact, almost all of the more than 270 scripts he read in search of his next project were "street" pictures. Instead, Mann wanted something completely different. Something unreal. Something that told its story in an almost Expressionistic way, like Gabriel García Márquez' *One Hundred Years Of Solitude*. He finally found what he was looking for in *The Keep*, a best-selling pulp horror novel set in World War Two that had been optioned by producers Gene Kirkwood and Howard W Koch, Jr., and set up at Paramount. They believed more in the premise than the actual story and when Mann agreed with them, the project was launched.

The Keep (1983)

Directed by Michael Mann. Screenplay by Michael Mann, based on the novel by F Paul Wilson.

The Cast: Scott Glenn (Glaeken Trismegestus), Alberta Watson (Eva Cuza), Jurgen Prochnow (Captain Woermann), Robert Prosky (Father Fonescu), Gabriel Byrne (Major Kaempffer), Ian McKellen (Dr Theodore Cuza), Michael Carter (Molasar)

The Crew: Produced by Gene Kirkwood and Howard W. Koch, Jr. Music by Tangerine Dream. Photographed by Alex Thomson, BSC. Edited by Dov Hoenig. Production Designed by John Box. Special Effects by Nick Allder. Visual Effects Supervised by Wally Veevers. Creature Designed by Nick Maley. Optical Effects by Peter Kuran and Visual Concepts Engineering. 96 minutes.

The Coverage: In the Fall of 1941, a Wehrmacht detachment led by Captain Woermann arrives at a pass in the Carpathian Alps in Romania. Their assignment is to guard the pass, and to do so, they will occupy a keep there. When they enter, the caretaker, Alexandru, tells them first that he and his family have always taken care of the keep and second that they should not stay there – no one ever stays there. When Woermann asks, "What drives people out in the middle of a rainy night?"

Alexandru answers: "Dreams." As he continues his examination of the keep, Woermann notices that all of the small stones are on the outside, while the larger stones are on the inside. It has been constructed backwards – not to keep people out, like a fort, but, rather, to keep something in. Suddenly, Alexandru notices one of the soldiers, Private Lutz, attempting to remove one of the many crosses built into the walls of the keep. He thinks they are made of silver. Woermann tells him that the crosses are all made of nickel and he punishes Lutz by giving him an assignment on first watch. Alexandru warns Woermann that they should never touch the crosses. That night, Lutz examines one cross in particular and realizes that while the others may be made of nickel, this one is indeed silver and he enlists the aid of a fellow soldier, Oster, to help him remove the cross. As they do so, the block in which the cross is mounted begins to come out of the wall. Rocket scientists that they are, they figure that if the block moves, then behind this one block there must be more silver. Once they get the block free, Lutz works his way down a narrow passage and finds another block and another silver cross. Pushing this block away, Lutz descends farther into the passageway and soon finds himself overlooking a gigantic chamber, as big as the entire mountain itself. Then, from within the darkness, glowing energy beams come together and shoot up toward Lutz, turning him instantly into charcoal. As Oster pulls what's left of his body from the passageway, the whole wall erupts and come apart. Like Lutz, Oster is suddenly turned to charcoal and his body bursts into nothing but dry black pieces. In Greece, Glaeken awakens, his eyes glowing, a cloud of energy like fireflies floating down onto his bed. Immediately, he gets up, wraps a mysterious box, gets dressed and departs. He heads to the docks where he hires a boat to take him to Romania. Back at the village outside the keep, Major Kaempffer and a squad of SS. arrive and immediately line three villagers up and machine-gun them. Kaempffer announces to the rest of the villagers that partisan activity will stop and that if it does not, he will continue machine-gunning villagers until it does. He then continues into the keep. Woermann chases him inside and tells him that whatever is killing his soldiers, it is not partisans. He believes that "something has been released." Kaempffer scoffs at this notion. But just then, soldiers arrive to tell Woermann that they have found "the rest of" Steiner. Woermann takes Kaempffer to see what he's talking about. This time, though, there's a new twist: writing on the wall in some sort of language that Alexandru the caretaker and Father Fonescu, the village parson, cannot interpret. When Kaempffer pushes him for a translation, Father Fonescu says there is only one person who might be able to translate the writing: Dr Theodore Cuza, a man who once made a study of the keep. When Kaempffer asks him where this Cuza might be, Fonescu tells him that Dr Cuza is Jewish, so he is "wherever you have taken the Jews." In a detainment camp, Dr Cuza waits along with his daughter Eva. Cuza is confined to a wheelchair, the victim of a disease that ages him prematurely. So although he is only in his 40s, his body is that of a 70-year-old. Meanwhile, in the forest somewhere, Glaeken rides his motorcycle toward the keep. When stopped by soldiers at a checkpoint and told to open his mysterious box, Glaeken tells them not to touch the box. And when his eyes flash with a mysterious purple light, the soldiers back away in fear. Back at the keep, Dr Cuza is escorted to the mysterious writing. He explains that it says, "I will be free." This convinces Kaempffer that partisans are indeed responsible for what's going on, until, that is, Dr Cuza tells him that the words are in a language that's been dead for 500 years. In their room, Father Fonescu meets with Dr Cuza and his daughter. Dr Cuza can hardly believe how Father Fonescu managed to rescue them from their certain death in the camps. Did he put the writing on the wall? No. Later, Eva goes to the mess hall to get food. She arouses the soldiers with her appearance, and as she makes her way back through the keep, she is grabbed by two men and sexually assaulted. But before the men can finish, the mysterious energy force we previously saw suddenly shoots down the hall and turns both of these men into charcoal. Eva passes out and the mysterious force now carries her back to her father. When Dr Cuza sees the giant, he is overcome with concern for his daughter. He wants to know what this thing has done to her. Suddenly, the force lays a glowing hand on Dr Cuza, shocking him unconscious with a burst of energy. Back in the forest, Glaeken continues toward the keep. When Eva awakens, she discovers that her father has somehow been partially healed. He can hardly believe it. He knows that the thing inside the keep is responsible. Just then, Woermann arrives and tells

Eva to pack her belongings. He wants to get her out of the keep and to the inn in the village where at least she will be safe from the men. Dr Cuza tells her to go. She arrives at the inn and as she enters her room with the innkeeper, they discover Glaeken already inside. He asks if this is the only room in the inn that overlooks the keep. When he is told it is, he says he will take it and when the innkeeper says that he has already rented it to Eva Cuza, Glaeken says she can stay there with him. Hypnotized by the mysterious Glaeken, Eva not only stays with him but allows herself to be seduced by him as well. Back in the keep, healed to the point that he can walk, Dr Cuza wanders the halls in search of the energy force. He finds it in a deserted hall and sees that it is more complete – no longer just an imploding cloud of energy, the thing has taken greater physical form, now appearing as a huge being with glowing red eyes and exposed musculature. The creature, named Molasar, wonders why Dr Cuza has such an air of death about him and when Dr Cuza explains that it must be because he was just in a death camp where people are murdered *en masse*, Molasar gets very upset. He wants to know who is murdering his people. Dr Cuza tells him that the soldiers in black are responsible. Molasar tells Dr Cuza he wants to destroy them but that he can't leave the keep until someone helps him remove the source of his power and hides it in the mountains. When Molasar asks Dr Cuza for his help in accomplishing this, he agrees immediately. He touches Dr Cuza again, jolting him with another blast of healing energy. Father Fonescu now confronts Dr Cuza about what's going on inside the keep. Dr Cuza tells him that he has made a deal that will save the world. But Father Fonescu tells Dr Cuza that he has made a deal with the devil and that he can burn in hell for all he cares now. Fonescu flees the keep. Eva now goes to the keep to get her father and when she brings him back to the inn, Glaeken emerges and tells Dr Cuza that he knows all about his deal with Molasar. Furthermore, Glaeken tells him, Molasar is lying. What he wants removed from the keep is not, as he said, the source of his power. It is instead what keeps him there and that if it is removed, Molasar will be released into the world of men. Dr Cuza doesn't think that's so bad and when he returns to the keep, he tells Kaempffer that there is a man at the inn who may be responsible for what's going on there. Back at the inn, Eva confronts Glaeken about his role in what is happening. He tells her that he has come to destroy Molasar. Just then, a detachment of SS troops bursts into the room and takes Glaeken hostage. As they haul him towards the keep, he struggles and they promptly machine-gun him. Bleeding fluorescent green blood from his bullet wounds, Glaeken plummets over a cliff edge and becomes lodged on an outcropping of rock. Inside the keep, Kaempffer shoots and kills Woermann and then discovers that every other soldier there has been turned into charcoal. Molasar emerges from the shadows and kills Kaempffer as well. Taking Dr Cuza deep into the keep, Molasar directs him in the removal of the talisman. Outside, Glaeken awakens and climbs out of the chasm. Returning to his room at the inn, he at last opens his mysterious box and removes a glowing red rod. Meanwhile, Eva enters the keep and confronts her father, trying to tell him not to do what Molasar says. Dr Cuza knocks his daughter to the ground and lifts his hand to strike her. Behind him, Molasar tells Dr Cuza to kill her. And with that, Dr Cuza suddenly realizes that Molasar is not what he says. Angrily, Molasar strikes Dr Cuza down, returning him to his unhealed state. Just then, Glaeken arrives. Taking the talisman, he attaches it to his rod. Purple energy blasts from the rod and bounces off all the crosses inside the keep, pushing Molasar back into the wall where he came from. As Glaeken is sucked away with Molasar, the villagers emerge to help Eva carry her father from the keep.

Research: In spite of the unrealistic nature of his story, Mann began working on *The Keep* with his usual exhaustive pre-production research. On *Thief*, he had relied on officers in the Chicago Police Department to serve as his technical advisors. But *The Keep* was completely different. One can't exactly shoot a documentary about a monster. Instead, Mann wanted to tell a fairy tale, a story that had about it the air of memories, dreams and nightmares. So it's appropriate then that the first element of Mann's research centered on a memory of his own: his 1969 meeting with Otto Skorzeny. Skorzeny, a former member of the SS, was one of World War Two's most successful commandos, known mostly for leading the raid that had rescued Mussolini from Italy in 1943. At Nuremberg, he conducted his own defense and earned an acquittal. After the war, he had run a mercenary operation out of Spain. At the time of their meeting, Mann was a self-described "nice Jewish kid from Chicago." What struck Mann about Skorzeny, however, was that he wasn't the kind of man who had or would have engaged in Dachau-style activities. But he nonetheless had joined the SS and fought for the Nazis. Haunted by that meeting – and his fascination with Skorzeny's psychology – Mann augmented his research by next reading the Walter Langdon Report, the document commissioned by the OSS to psychoanalyze Hitler. Langdon, a doctor from New York, had talked to many people who had known Hitler in the years preceding the war. Mann saw this report as not just about the psychosis of one man, but also about the psychosis of a whole nation – a whole time. This "dark side," as Mann called it, formed the foundation of his screenplay. Taking next a page from Bruno Bettelheim's classic, *The Uses Of Enchantment*, Mann combined all these ideas about the emotions, psychology and politics of the time and encoded them into a simple story that relies on feeling for its effectiveness rather than on concrete explanations.

Story: Once again, the central factor in Mann's story is a dangerous deal undertaken for gain. And while *Thief* redressed the Faust legend in mobster clothes, *The Keep* takes it literally into the supernatural realm. That Cuza – a Jew, no less! – makes a deal first with Molasar and then with the SS is really the ultimate 20th-century statement about the seduction of power. As they had inside Folsom and on the streets of Chicago, deals fill the keep: Cuza and Molasar; Father Fonescu and Cuza; Lutz and Oster; Glaeken and Eva. Each of these people align themselves with others and learn, only too late, that to rely on something beyond their control is to court self-destruction. It's an end met by nearly everyone in the film. And in a beautiful gender inversion of the story of Abraham and Isaac, Cuza is driven to the point of almost killing his only daughter. Talk about self-destruction! The only thing that saves him, of course, is the fact that he is a Mann Man.

The Mann Man: Like Murphy and Frank before him, Cuza is a dedicated man who nearly sells his soul to achieve something he thinks he wants. And like Murphy and Frank, he undergoes an epiphany that drives him back to the truth. But what's interesting here is the way in which Mann retains this central notion even though the surfaces of the stories couldn't be more dissimilar. Like Murphy and Frank, Cuza is a prisoner. When we first meet him, he is on his way to a concentration camp. But Cuza also is a prisoner in his own body and this imprisonment has created a need for something larger. So that while Frank was in a sense crippled inside, Cuza is crippled outside. And while Frank wants a perfect life for himself, Cuza dreams of saving a whole nation. Both men then form attachments with forces beyond their control to achieve their dreams. Mann seems to be telling us that it doesn't matter what your dreams are, exactly: if you are selling yourself to achieve them, they can't be worthwhile.

Design: Working with such an unrealistic story, Mann had the opportunity to design his production and create things in a way that he hadn't yet. On *Thief*, tools and guns were simply brought in by people who had used them and used again. But *The Keep* meant creating everything from scratch. The first step was to find a location that could serve as the mountain pass housing the keep. After location scouting in Romania turned up nothing usable, Mann asked experts at a nearby university to use their geology computer to help him find what he was looking for. Working from a list of longitudes and latitudes, Mann finally settled on an abandoned slate quarry in Wales. At 100 feet deep and with walls that were as black as if they had been painted, the location was perfect. Using architecture to underscore the polar nature of the film, Mann and production designer John Box designed the village and the keep as opposites. The village is thus very bright and white while the keep itself is almost completely black. And while the village seems to be dripping with moisture (and, by extension, life), the inside of the keep is extremely dry. So dry, in fact, that even death itself is dry. Drawing on photos of corpses from World War Two, Mann directed the head of his special effects department, Nick Allder, to come up with something similar. The result is completely unique. Molasar dispatches the Nazis by turning their bodies into blackened brittle masses of charcoal without a drop of blood in sight. While Molasar in the source novel does not undergo any evolutionary changes, Mann's approach was different and again design was employed to underscore this thematic idea. For Mann, Molasar is the ultimate evil and he gains substance as the story progresses because this is what evil does – it is a psychosis turned into politics. The first stage, depicting Molasar as a glowing brain within a cloud of imploding particles, was accomplished by building a 14-foot,

3,500-pound body full of metal pores through which steam was passed. By reversing and then optically enhancing that footage, the imploding energy cloud was perfectly realized. In the second stage, after Molasar had gained some form, Mann designed the back of his head so that its shape resembled an Austrian helmet circa World War One. All of this "tricky visual language," as Mann called it, may pass by some viewers unaware, but he deemed it better than relying on dialogue.

Shooting And Cutting: To further enhance the polar qualities of the village and the keep, each location was exposed differently. In the village, exposures were set for shadows so that the sunlit highlights were burned out and overexposed. In the keep, exposures were set for the highlights so that everything in shadow quickly became a pit of impenetrable darkness. This effect was further enhanced by lighting the inside of the keep only with very defined shafts of light, their particular color and effect achieved by employing arc lamps that had been built in the 1920s and 1930s.

Music: Again Mann refused to employ a traditional orchestral score and instead relied on Tangerine Dream to provide him with the musical underpinning for his story. While with *Thief*, their electronic instruments reflected Frank's own equipment, here the effect is more of temporal dislocation. Mann's story is out of time and the score contributes to this impression.

The Final Word: Upon its initial release, the *Variety* reviewer asked, "How do these dogs get made?" and pointed to the film as proof of the "one-step-forward, two-steps-back career theory." *The Keep* went on to become not only a box office disaster, earning just $1.2 million in its initial US theatrical run, but a critical failure as well. All of which strikes one as curious when viewing the film again, especially in the context of Mann's work as a whole. As of this writing, only the pan-and-scan version remains in print on home video with no plans for a reissue on DVD. It's a shame, because seen in its original widescreen format, the movie is a revelation, testimony to Mann's mastery even then of the anamorphic format that has since become his exclusive working medium. This is an overlooked masterpiece whose reassessment is long past due. In the meantime, get your hands on the ultra-rare laserdisc. Position on the Mann Top Ten List: #5.

NB: The last name of the character played by Scott Glenn – Trismegestus – is the Greek word for 'harvest'. The death of special effects wizard Wally Veevers (*The Keep* was his last film) delayed the production by six months. This is the only Mann film with any nudity.

5. Return To TV-Land

Ask the average film and TV buff who created *Miami Vice* and you'll probably get "Michael Mann" for an answer. So prevalent is this misconception that some home-video releases of Mann's movies actually say "From the creator of *Miami Vice*" on them! A common Hollywood legend about the show's inception goes like this: at a dinner party one night, Brandon Tartikoff (then president of NBC) handed Mann a napkin with "MTV cops" written on it. True or not, the series was in fact the brainchild of Anthony Yerkovich who, like Mann, got his start in episodic television (as a writer and producer of *Hill Street Blues*). However, there can be little doubt that most of *Miami Vice* has got Mann's hand in it. From the importation of Mel Bourne, his production designer on *Thief*, to the Tangerine Dream-style music of Jan Hammer, *Miami Vice* is definitely a Michael Mann production.

Miami Vice (1984-1989)

Directed by Thomas Carter, Abel Ferrara, Rob Cohen, Christopher Crowe, Paul Michael Glaser, Ate de Jong, Paul Krasny, Aaron Lipstadt, Edward James Olmos, David Soul, Don Johnson, Michael Mann. Written by Anthony Yerkovich, Michael Duggan, Peter Lance, Michael Mann.

The Cast: Don Johnson ("Sonny" Crockett), Philip Michael Thomas (Ricardo Tubbs), Edward James Olmos (Martin Castillo), Saundra Santiago (Gina Calabrese), Olivia Brown (Trudy Joplin), Michael Talbott (Stanley Switek), John Diehl (Larry Zito), Martin Ferrero (Izzy Moreno), Sheena Easton (Caitlin Davies-Crockett), Pam Grier (Valerie Gordon).

Guest Stars Worth Looking For: Julia Roberts, Bruce Willis, Ving Rhames, Laurence Fishburne, Michael DeLorenzo, Giancarlo Esposito, Joe Morton, Jay O Sanders, Garcelle Beauvais, Joan Chen, Gary Cole, Richard Belzer, Cleavant Derricks, Lou Diamond Phillips, Viggo Mortensen, Annette Bening, Ron Perlman, John Leguizamo, Bill Paxton, Wesley Snipes, Stanley Tucci, Liam Neeson, Jeff Fahey, Oliver Platt, Laura San Giacomo, Melissa Leo, Robert Joy, Michael Madsen,

John Turturro, Penn Jillette, Gene Simmons, Glenn Frey, Eartha Kitt, Power Station, Little Richard, David Johansen, Frankie Valli, Miles Davis, El DeBarge, Phil Collins, Ted Nugent, Jan Hammer, Fiona, Leonard Cohen, Frank Zappa, Willie Nelson, Vanity, Isaac Hayes, James Brown, Michael DesBarres, Lee Iacocca, Iman, Tommy Chong, Barbra Streisand, Carlos Palomino, Roberto Duran, Mark Breland, Randall "Tex" Cobb, Bill Russell, Bernard King, G Gordon Liddy

The Crew: Created by Anthony Yerkovich. Produced by John Nicolella, Michael Attanasio, Richard Brams, Dick Wolf, Michael Mann. Music by Jan Hammer, Tim Truman. Photographed by Robert Collins, Duke Callaghan, James Contner, Tom Priestly, Jr., Oliver Wood. Edited by David Rosenbloom, Buford Hayes, Douglas Ibold, Richard Leeman. Visual Consultant Mel Bourne. Art Direction by Todd Hallowell

The Final Word: Mann was working on the script for *Manhunter* when he received a teleplay titled *Gold Coast* from his agent. At first, he wondered why his agent was even suggesting he consider going back into television. But he insisted that Mann simply read the script and once he did, he wondered how he could get it away and make it as a movie. When he couldn't, he instead became the show's executive producer, changing the title to *Miami Vice* and imprinting it with everything he had learned from his big-screen theatrical experiences. Unlike other TV producers, Mann treated the shows as if they were movies, doing many things that in the feature film world would be the job of the director. He set the look of the show – based on a trip to the paint store one day where he experimented with pastel colors until he found some interesting combinations – deciding even such things as what kind of cars the characters should drive and involving himself with the editing. To Mann, of course, this style was not gratuitous, but was instead "an expression of place and content, the milieu the guys are moving through." Perhaps even more indicative of that milieu than the sets and costumes was the soundtrack, probably the show's greatest achievement. Combining the theme music and underscore of Jan Hammer (who entered the picture when Tangerine Dream turned the offer down) with pre-existing pop songs to comment on the action, the result was so successful at the time that it has since become a cliché. But who can forget the Phil Collins hit "I Can Feel It In The Air Tonight" backing up Crockett and Tubbs on their way to a final showdown in the pilot episode? Nominated twenty times for an Emmy Award and winning four, *Miami Vice* was a huge success in every sense of the word, a show that has entered the cultural mindscape and remains lodged there to this day. Position on the Mann Top Ten List: #8.

N.B.: Debuting on NBC on September 16, 1984, *Miami Vice* ran for five seasons, totaling 110 episodes. The final episode aired on May 21, 1989. A missing episode not broadcast during the regular run (*Too Much, Too Late*) was aired on January 25, 1990. Miguel Pinero, who played Calderon, is an ex-con turned playwright whose off-Broadway play *Short Eyes* won an Obie and a New York Drama Critics Circle award. Crockett's yacht was called The St Vitus' Dance. The song 'Cold Wind Blows' by Karla Bonoff was exclusively recorded for the episode *Bought And Paid For* and has never been released in any form.

Complete Episode Guide

Season One

September 16, 1984 *Miami Vice* (aka *Brother's Keeper*)

September 28, 1984 *Heart Of Darkness*

October 5, 1984 *Cool Runnin'*

October 19, 1984 *Hit List*

October 26, 1984 *Calderon's Demise*

November 2, 1984 *One-Eyed Jack*

November 9, 1984 *No Exit*

November 16, 1984 *The Great McCarthy*

November 30, 1984 *Glades*

December 7, 1984 *Give A Little, Take A Little*

December 14, 1984 *Little Prince*

January 4, 1985 *Milk Run*

January 11, 1985 *Score*

January 18, 1985 *Golden Triangle*

February 1, 1985 *Smuggler's Blues*

February 8, 1985 *Rites Of Passage*

February 22, 1985 *The Maze*
March 8, 1985 *Made For Each Other*
March 15, 1985 *The Home Invaders*
March 29, 1985 *Nobody Lives Forever*
May 3, 1985 *Evan*
May 10, 1985 *Lombard*

Season Two

September 27, 1985 *The Prodigal Son*
October 4, 1985 *Whatever Works*
October 18, 1985 *Out Where The Buses Don't Run*
October 25, 1985 *The Dutch Oven*
November 1, 1985 *Buddies*
November 8, 1985 *Junk Love*
November 15, 1985 *Tale Of The Goat*
November 22, 1985 *Bushido*
November 29, 1985 *Bought And Paid For*
December 6, 1985 *Back In The World*
December 13, 1985 *Phil The Shill*
January 10, 1986 *Definitely Miami*
January 17, 1986 *Yankee Dollar*
January 24, 1986 *One Way Ticket*
January 31, 1986 *Little Miss Dangerous*
February 14, 1986 *Florence Italy*
February 21, 1986 *French Twist*
March 7, 1986 *The Fix*
March 14, 1986 *Payback*
April 4, 1986 *Free Verse*
May 2, 1986 *Trust Fund Pirates*
May 9, 1986 *Sons And Lovers*

Season Three

September 26, 1986 *When Irish Eyes Are Crying*
October 3, 1986 *Stone's War*
October 10, 1986 *Kill Shot*

October 17, 1986 *Walk-Alone*
October 24, 1986 *The Good Collar*
October 31, 1986 *Shadow In The Dark*
November 7, 1986 *El Viejo*
November 14, 1986 *Better Living Through Chemistry*
November 21, 1986 *Baby Blues*
December 5, 1986 *Streetwise*
December 12, 1986 *Forgive Us Our Debts*
January 9, 1987 *Down For The Count* (part 1)
January 16, 1987 *Down For The Count* (part 2)
January 23, 1987 *Cuba Libre*
February 6, 1987 *The Savage*
February 13, 1987 *Theresa*
February 20, 1987 *The Afternoon Plane*
February 27, 1987 *Lend Me An Ear*
March 13, 1987 *Red Tape*
March 20, 1987 *By Hooker By Crook*
March 27, 1987 *Knock Knock...Who's There?*
April 3, 1987 *Viking Bikers From Hell*
May 1, 1987 *Everybody's In Showbiz*
May 8, 1987 *Heroes Of The Revolution*

Season Four

September 25, 1987 *Contempt Of Court*
October 2, 1987 *Amen...Send Money*
October 16, 1987 *Death And The Lady*
October 23, 1987 *The Big Thaw*
October 30, 1987 *Child's Play*
November 6, 1987 *God's Work*
November 13, 1987 *Missing Hours*
November 20, 1987 *Like A Hurricane*
December 4, 1987 *The Rising Sun Of Death*
January 15, 1988 *Love At First Sight*
January 22, 1988 *Rock And A Hard Place*
February 5, 1988 *The Cows Of October*
February 12, 1988 *Vote Of Confidence*

February 19, 1988 *Baseballs Of Death*
February 26, 1988 *Indian Wars*
March 4, 1988 *Honor Among Thieves?*
March 11, 1988 *Hell Hath No Fury*
March 18, 1988 *Badge Of Dishonor*
April 1, 1988 *Blood And Roses*
April 15, 1988 *A Bullet For Crockett*
April 29, 1988 *Deliver Us From Evil*
May 6, 1988 *Mirror Image*

Season Five

November 4, 1988 *Hostile Takeover*
November 11, 1988 *Redemption In Blood*
November 18, 1988 *Heart Of Night*
December 2, 1988 *Bad Timing*
December 9, 1988 *Borrasca*
December 16, 1988 *Line Of Fire*
January 13, 1989 *Asian Cut*
January 20, 1989 *Hard Knocks*
February 3, 1989 *Fruit Of The Poison Tree*
February 10, 1989 *To Have And To Hold*
February 17, 1989 *Miami Squeeze*
March 3, 1989 *Jack Of All Trades*
March 10, 1989 *The Cell Within*
March 17, 1989 *The Lost Madonna*
April 28, 1989 *Over The Line*
May 5, 1989 *Victims Of Circumstance*
June 14, 1989 *World Of Trouble*
June 21, 1989 *Miracle Man*
June 28, 1989 *Leap Of Faith*
May 21, 1989 *Freefall* (Finale)
Missing Episode not broadcast by NBC *Too Much, Too Late*

Emmy Awards and Nominations

Season One

Winner for Outstanding Supporting Actor in a Drama Series (Edward James Olmos)

Nominated for Outstanding Lead Actor in a Drama Series (Don Johnson)

Nominated for Outstanding Drama Series (Michael Mann, Executive Producer; Anthony Yerkovich, Executive Producer; John Nicolella, Supervising Producer; Liam O'Brien, Supervising Producer; John Nicolella, Producer; Mel Swope, Producer; Richard Brams, Co-Producer; George E Crosby, Co-Producer)

Brother's Keeper

Winner for Outstanding Cinematography for a Series (Bob Collins, Cinematographer)

Winner for Outstanding Film Sound Editing for a Series (Chuck Moran, Supervising Sound Editor; Bruce Bell, Sound Editor; Victor B Lackey, Sound Editor; Ian MacGregor-Scott, Sound Editor; Carl Mahakian, Sound Editor; John Oettinger, Sound Editor; Bernie Pincus, Sound Editor; Warren Smith, Sound Editor; Bruce Stambler, Sound Editor; Mike Wilhoit, Sound Editor; Kyle Wright, Sound Editor; Paul Wittenberg, ADR Editor; Jerry Sanford Cohen, Music Editor)

Nominated for Outstanding Writing in a Drama Series (Anthony Yerkovich, Writer)

Cool Runnin'

Nominated for Outstanding Directing in a Drama Series (Lee H Katzin, Director)

No Exit

Winner for Outstanding Art Direction for a Series (Jeffrey Howard, Art Director; Robert Lacey, Set Decorator)

Nominated for Outstanding Cinematography for a Series (A J "Duke" Callaghan, Cinematographer)

Nominated for Outstanding Costume Design for a Series (Jodie Tillen, Costume Designer)

Smuggler's Blues

Nominated for Outstanding Directing in a Drama Series (Paul Michael Glaser, Director)

Nominated for Outstanding Film Editing for a Series (Michael B Hoggan)

Nominated for Outstanding Sound Mixing in a Drama Series (John A Larsen, Supervising Sound Editor; Scott Hecker, Sound Editor; Harry B Miller III, Sound Editor; Robert Rutledge, Sound Editor; Gary Vaughan, Sound Editor; Jay Wilkinson, Sound Editor; Norto Sepulveda, ADR Editor; Jerry Sanford Cohen, Music Editor)

Evan

Nominated for Outstanding Achievement in Music Composition for a Series (dramatic underscore) (Jan Hammer, Composer)

Nominated for Outstanding Film Editing for a Series (Robert A Daniels, Editor)

Season Two

Nominated for Outstanding Supporting Actor in a Drama Series (Edward James Olmos)

Out Where The Buses Don't Run

Nominated for Outstanding Editing for a Series (single camera production) (Robert A Daniels, Editor)

Bushido

Nominated for Outstanding Achievement in Music Composition for a Series (dramatic underscore) (Jan Hammer, Composer)

Florence, Italy

Nominated for Outstanding Sound Mixing in a Drama Series (Rick Alexander, Sound Mixer; Anthony Costantini, Sound Mixer; Daniel Leahy, Sound Mixer; Mike Tromer, Sound Mixer)

Season Four

Like A Hurricane

Nominated for Outstanding Sound Mixing in a Drama Series (Ray West, Sound Mixer; Joe Citarella, Sound Mixer; Grover Helsley, Sound Mixer; Joe Foglia, Sound Mixer)

Concurrently with his producing chores on *Miami Vice*, Mann set up another TV series, *Crime Story* – a show about a crusading detective with a personalized sense of justice based on the real-life experiences of Chuck Adamson, the former Chicago police officer who had served as one of the technical advisors on *Thief*. But as sure as he was that *Miami Vice* would be a hit, Mann wasn't sure if *Crime Story* would be. The one thing he did know: he loved the concept.

Crime Story (1986-1988)

Directed by Abel Ferrara, Colin Bucksey, Mimi Leder, Aaron Lipstadt, Gary Sinise, David Soul, Michael Mann. Written by Chuck Adamson, David Burke, Gustave Reininger, Peter Lance.

The Cast: Dennis Farina (Mike Torrello), Anthony John Denison (Ray Luca), David Caruso (Johnny O'Donnell), Darlanne Fluegel (Julie Torrello), Stephen Lang (David Abrams), Ted Levine (Frank Holman), Bill Smitrovich (Danny Krycheck), John Santucci (Pauli Taglia), Andrew Dice Clay (Max Goldman)

Guest Stars Worth Looking For: Julia Roberts, Kevin Spacey, Eric Bogosian, Ving Rhames, Pam Grier

The Crew: Created by Chuck Adamson and Gustave Reininger. Produced by Ervin Zavada, Stuart Cohen, Gail Morgan Hickman. Edited by Jack Hofstra, Terence Anderson. Music by Todd Rundgren. Photographed by James Contner, Ronald Garcia. Production Designed by Gregory Bolton, Stephen Dane, Hilda Stark.

The Final Word: Directed by Abel Ferrara with a blistering score by Todd Rundgren, and a smoldering performance by Dennis Farina as Mike Torrello, the two-hour pilot for *Crime Story* stands alone as a great movie all by itself. It's a shame when viewed in the context of the remaining episodes of the show. The first season promised so much, but the second season deteriorated when most of the original writers headed for the new CBS smash *Wiseguy*. The show changed its look as well and then changed locales – from Chicago to Las Vegas and finally, in the last four episodes of the second season, to Mexico. But all the blame can hardly be laid at Mann's door. His original vision for the show was as an epic mini-series. He wanted to have an established beginning, middle and end and he wanted to follow that arc over the course of a full season. He never wanted it to go on. NBC, of course, had only *Miami Vice* on the brain and they wanted it to be open-ended. As a result, the show – as David Lynch's *Twin Peaks* would after it – suffered from being forced to sustain itself. Nonetheless, *Crime Story* struck a deeper chord with some viewers who preferred it over that other Michael Mann show. The end result is a series that is well worth flipping over to when you see it in syndication, but it's the pilot (now on DVD) that's a must have for your Mann collection. Position on the Mann Top Ten List: #7.

NB: Debuting on NBC on September 18, 1986, *Crime Story* ran for two seasons, totaling 42 episodes. The final episode aired on May 10, 1988. *Crime Story* creator Chuck Adamson appeared in *Thief* as the police sergeant who talks to Frank at the station after Urizzi has brought him in for a beating. Bill Hanhardt, the legendary detective who ran the Criminal Investigative Unit of the Chicago Police Department in the 1960s, served as consultant on *Crime Story*. In 2000, he was arrested by the FBI for masterminding one of the largest jewel-theft rings in the nation. The safe-cracking job Luca and his gang pull off in the pilot episode is almost a shot-for-shot lift of the LA score from *Thief*, burning bar and all.

Complete Episode Guide

Season One

September 18, 1986 *Crime Story*
September 19, 1986 *Final Transmission*
September 26, 1986 *Shadow Dancer*
September 30, 1986 *The Saint Louis Book Of Blues*
October 7, 1986 *The War*
October 14, 1986 *Abrams For The Defense*
October 28, 1986 *Pursuit Of A Wanted Felon*
November 4, 1986 *Old Friends, Dead Ends*
November 11, 1986 *Justice Hits The Skids*
December 5, 1986 *For Love Or Money*

December 12, 1986 *Hide And Go Thief*
December 26, 1986 *Strange Bedfellows*
January 9, 1987 *Fatal Crossroads* (aka *Fortune in Men's Eyes*)
January 16, 1987 *Torrello On Trial*
January 30, 1987 *Kingdom Of Money*
February 6, 1987 *The Battle Of Las Vegas*
February 13, 1987 *The Survivor*
February 27, 1987 *The Pinnacle*
March 6, 1987 *Top Of The World* (aka *The King In A Cage*)
March 13, 1987 *Ground Zero*

Season Two

September 22, 1987 *The Senator, The Movie Star And The Mob*
September 29, 1987 *Blast From The Past*
October 20, 1987 *Always A Blonde*
October 27, 1987 *Atomic Fallout*
November 3, 1987 *Shockwaves*
November 10, 1987 *Robbery, Armed*
November 24, 1987 *Little Girl Lost*
December 8, 1987 *Love Hurts*
December 15, 1987 *MIG-21*
January 5, 1988 *Moulin Rouge*
January 12, 1988 *Seize The Time*
January 19, 1988 *Femme Fatale*
February 2, 1988 *Protected Witness*
February 9, 1988 *Last Rites*
March 8, 1988 *Pauli Taglia's Dream*
March 15, 1988 *Roadrunner*
March 22, 1988 *Desert Justice* (aka *The Brothel Wars*)
March 29, 1988 *Byline*
April 5, 1988 *The Hearings*
April 26, 1988 *Pursuit*
May 3, 1988 *Escape*
May 10, 1988 *Going Home*

6. Just You And Me Now, Sport

Before the phenomenal success of both *Miami Vice* and *Crime Story*, Mann had already signed on for his next feature, a film version of the 1981 best-seller *Red Dragon*, by Thomas Harris. Similar to *The Home Invaders*, *Red Dragon* is a book built on reality. Mann spent three years adapting it in his trademark style, applying the same approach to police work in *Manhunter* as he had to criminal activity in *Thief*. The result is almost science fiction-like in execution and although not successful in its first run, the film has since been tagged as the forerunner to nearly every other serial killer movie that followed.

Manhunter (1986)

Directed by Michael Mann. Screenplay by Michael Mann, based on *Red Dragon* by Thomas Harris.

The Cast: William Petersen (Will Graham), Kim Greist (Molly Graham), Joan Allen (Reba), Brian Cox (Hannibal Lecter), Dennis Farina (Jack Crawford), Stephen Lang (Freddie Lounds), Tom Noonan (Francis Dollarhyde)

The Crew: Produced by Dino De Laurentiis, Richard A Roth and Bernard Williams. Music by The Reds and Michel Rubini. Photographed by Dante Spinotti. Edited by Dov Hoenig. Production Designed by Mel Bourne. Visual Consultant Gusmano Cesaretti. 119 minutes. Director's Cut runs 124 minutes.

The Coverage: FBI Agent Jack Crawford visits retired FBI Agent Will Graham at his home in Florida. Graham, a celebrated detective with an uncanny ability to catch serial killers, quit his job after nearly being killed by his last arrest, the notorious Dr Hannibal "The Cannibal" Lecter. But a new killer is on the loose – operating on a lunar cycle – and Crawford wants Graham to come back and help him catch the killer before the next full moon, and he shows him pictures of the two families already slaughtered by the killer to arouse his sympathies. Graham says he'll think about it. While Graham's son, Kevin, helps him erect a fence to keep crabs from getting turtle eggs, Graham's wife, Molly, berates Crawford for asking him back to work. That night, Graham asks Molly what she thinks about him "just looking at evidence." She doesn't think he's really asking – she thinks he's already decided to go back. Taking on the case, Graham's first stop is the Leeds house, scene of the second murders. Graham enters the way the killer did, making notes to himself about the details of the crime into a tape recorder. Back at his hotel, Graham watches home movies of both families. He calls Molly and tells her he loves her, then returns to watching the tapes. Suddenly, he begins acting like the killer, talking to himself about how beautiful the women are. Then he has a breakthrough, deducing that the killer must have touched the women. Graham calls Crawford and tells him he wants Price, the FBI's fingerprint expert, to come to Atlanta and dust the eyeballs and nails of all the victims. At the headquarters of the Atlanta Police Department, the local authorities are smug to the intrusion of Crawford and Graham. After a mould of the killer's teeth is shown – reconstructed from bite marks on the female victims – Graham gives a statement in which he says he believes the killer is highly organized and probably responsible in his daily life. The Atlanta chief says, "In other words, he could be anybody?" Graham agrees. The police chief tells his officers to stop referring to the killer as "The Tooth Fairy," then sends them on their way. Outside, Freddie Lounds, reporter for *The National Tattler*, confronts Graham. Graham tells him to stay away, then tells Crawford that Lounds took pictures of him when he was in the hospital after Lecter stabbed him. Graham then tells Crawford he plans to visit Lecter so he can recover the mindset. Graham meets with Lecter and tells him he wants help catching The Tooth Fairy. Lecter agrees to help and Graham shows him the files. Lecter asks Graham if he knows how he caught him. Graham says he does not. To which Lecter replies, "You caught me because we're just alike, you and me." Graham flees Lecter's cell, only to have Lounds secretly take his picture outside. Meanwhile, Lecter makes a phone call, posing as a book publisher to get Graham's home address. On a plane to the next murder scene, Graham falls asleep while looking at forensics photos. He dreams of Molly but is awakened when the little girl next to him sees the brutal photos and bursts into tears. At the Jacobi house, Graham again acts like the killer, backing away from the house into the woods, trying to find a vantage point from which to see inside. When he spots a candy bar wrapper on the ground near a tree with a rope swing, Graham climbs into the tree and discovers that he not only has a perfect view, but that a branch has been cut away and that a strange Chinese character has been carved into the tree. With the police back on the scene, Graham calls Crawford and finds out that his picture is all over the *Tattler*. Just then, a security guard brings a note found in Lecter's cell to Dr Chilton. Chilton phones Graham and Crawford and reads the note. It's from The Tooth Fairy, all right. The note encourages Lecter to correspond, but part of the note is missing. Graham and Crawford fly the note to a forensics lab where they quickly analyze it for clues. They discover a hair but no fingerprints. Another scientist sees part of the missing piece, detailing how Lecter and The Tooth Fairy should communicate. It looks like they planned on using the *Tattler*. Crawford figures they must mean the personal ads and when they contact the *Tattler*, they find an ad from Lecter to The Tooth Fairy, but it's in code. Plans to substitute their own ad to lure The Tooth Fairy into a trap are dashed, however, when they find they can't break the code. If they run their own ad not in the right code, The Tooth Fairy will know the ad is not from Lecter. Graham says they should let the ad run, even though they don't know what it says. Then they can use Graham himself for bait. His psychiatrist, Dr Bloom, tells Graham he doesn't think that's a good idea, but Graham goes ahead with the plan anyway. Using Lounds, Graham tells lies designed to upset the killer, then poses for a photo in such a way that the location could be figured out by The Tooth Fairy. Graham then walks near the location. When someone approaches, Graham and the police quickly overtake him, but it's not the killer. Meanwhile, in a parking garage, The Tooth Fairy grabs Lounds and takes him to his house. There, the killer shows him pictures of his victims, then forces Lounds to read a statement. He then ties him to a wheelchair and sets him on fire. At the hospital, Graham and Crawford discover Lounds never regained consciousness. Crawford also tells Graham that they finally broke the code in Lecter's ad: he gave The Tooth Fairy Graham's home address and told him to kill them all. Molly and Kevin are immediately taken to a safe-house and when Graham takes Kevin to the grocery store, he asks about what happened to him before. Graham tells Kevin about being stabbed by Lecter. Molly asks Graham if he can quit but he says he can't. Graham heads off to catch the killer. Meanwhile, The Tooth Fairy, who we now learn is named Francis Dollarhyde, is at work at a film-processing lab. He meets Reba, a blind woman, and is attracted to her. Taking her home with him, he watches movies of his next victims and then Reba seduces him. Dollarhyde is in love. But when he goes to pick up Reba for another date the next night, he sees her with another man and goes crazy, killing the man and taking Reba to his house where he plans to kills her. Back in his office, Graham suddenly realizes that the killer knew so much about his victims because he had seen their home movies. Quickly checking into it, Crawford finds Graham is right – the home movies of both families were processed by the same lab. Getting on a plane, Graham and Crawford run driver's licences of lab employees and find a person with a physical description that matches what they know about the killer: Dollarhyde. Graham knows he's the one. The police scramble to the location and Graham kills Dollarhyde in a final shoot-out. Back on the beach at home, Graham and Kevin check the cage they had built to protect the turtle eggs and discover that because of their efforts, nearly all of the hatchlings have survived.

Research: With most of his characteristic research already in place thanks to the book, Mann had more to do in terms of creating a workable screenplay. Mann spoke briefly with Thomas Harris, the book's author, then set about making his own changes to the source novel. Most of these changes centered on the character of Dollarhyde, removing the scenes that were flashbacks to his abusive childhood (Mann felt they slowed the action down too much). Also removed were the lengthy explanations of the Red Dragon. He still managed to retain the Blake painting and the mah-jongg tile, but removed the rather incredible scene where Dollarhyde actually eats the Blake painting in an attempt to rid himself of the Red Dragon's influence. The only time Mann departs from the book in a major way is for the ending. In the novel, Dollarhyde fakes his own death by blowing up his house as the police close in, then reappears at Graham's house for a final duel. Perhaps Mann felt that such 'surprise' endings had already become a cliché and so elected to condense the climax. Besides, Mann's ending is much more in line with real police procedures than Harris' own shock for shock's sake finale.

As he had done with James Caan on *Thief*, Mann did not rehearse his lead actor but instead sent him to work with the Violent Crimes Unit of the Chicago Police Department and then for six weeks of training at Quantico with the FBI. So immersed did William Petersen become in his role that following the completion of shooting, he dyed his hair blonde to shock himself out of seeing Will Graham every time he looked in the mirror.

Story: Once again, the central conflict of the story is a dangerous deal. But while *The Jericho Mile* was about a 'bad' guy making a deal with the 'good' guys and *Thief* was about a 'bad' guy making a deal with 'bad' guys and *The Keep* was about a 'good' guy making a deal with a 'bad' guy, *Manhunter* is about a 'good' guy making a deal with other 'good' guys. In spite of this variation, however, the essential truth of Mann's philosophy remains the same: no matter which way you cut it, these deals are dangerous. The motivation matters very little because the problem centers on aligning yourself with forces beyond your control – even if they sometimes reside within. Graham may be motivated by wanting to do good, but he nearly destroys himself and his whole family in the process. And because there can be little doubt at the end of *Manhunter* that Graham will ever make such a deal again, he becomes yet another variation of the Mann Man.

The Mann Man: Like his cinematic brothers before him, Graham is a dedicated professional caught in a dangerous deal on his way to an epiphany. This time, however, Mann sees what happens when the attachments seek out the protagonist. Graham isn't interested in personal gain (like Frank) but is instead motivated by doing good (like Cuza). The interesting coda to this is the question never answered in *The Keep*: is it worth it? In other words, would Cuza's alignment with Molasar have been okay if it really had resulted in the destruction of the Nazis? In a similar fashion, we are left to ponder the cost of Graham's undertaking. He may have saved an innocent family, but what about what happened to his own family? This dehumanization of Graham combined with the humanization of Dollarhyde (accomplished by showing him having real feelings for Reba) results in characters that go against easy definitions of right and wrong or good and evil. Mann is telling us that there really isn't much of a difference between any of us.

As humans, we all have the same dreams and aspirations, we all want to be loved and admired for who we are, and we all want to do a good job. It's how we deal with these things that makes the difference. Graham may be like the killer, but he would never become one because he deals with these feelings in the right way. Similarly, Dollarhyde may be like Graham, but he will never become him because he cannot deal with his feelings in the right way. The only way out is for everyone to save themselves.

Design: Similar to *The Keep*, architecture becomes terribly important in *Manhunter* as either a direct reflection of or counterpoint to characters and events. Like the poles of the village and the keep, Graham, Dollarhyde and Lecter are similar opposites. For Mann, this was the most fascinating aspect of all of *Red Dragon* and he underscores it in a number of unique ways. First, Graham is depicted as inhabiting the workaday world. His discussion with his son about Lecter takes place in the aisles of a grocery store and when he stares at brutal crime scene photos, he does so on a plane next to a little girl and her mother. By contrast, Francis Dollarhyde works in a film-processing plant, a bizarre, windowless world in which light is, literally, dangerous. He passes through a door unlike anything we've seen before as he enters the appropriately titled 'darkroom'. His house, at the edge of a swamp and buried in the trees at the end of a long dirt road, is filled with images from outer space: enlarged photographs of the moon, the stars and the surface of Mars all contribute to our subconscious perception that this guy is really out there. In a unique flourish, the candy bar wrapper Graham finds on the ground behind the Jacobi house is a Mars bar, neatly tying into Dollarhyde's character even though neither we – nor Graham – know it at that point. It's completely appropriate in the context of what the movie is saying, therefore, that the safe-house Molly and Kevin are put into is almost an exact duplicate of Dollarhyde's house. It sits at the end of a long dirt road, buried in the trees, on the edge of water. One wall is even covered with a photographic mural, but instead of the surface of Mars (as in Dollarhyde's house), the picture is of a tropical beach. This careful design tells us that as Graham and Dollarhyde close in on each other, they become more and more alike. Similarly, Mann puts Lecter not in a dank dungeon (as Jonathan Demme would do so wrong-headedly in *The Silence Of The Lambs*) but rather in a completely white environment. He even wears white. Because of what we know about Lecter, white thus becomes black in our subconscious perception – the sign and substance of pure evil, an indicator of death. The master bedroom of the Leeds house is pure white. The interior and exterior of the Jacobi house is pure white. The doctors who take care of Lecter also wear white and inhabit white offices. The interior of the whole facility where Lecter is held is white. The note Dollarhyde sends to Lecter is written on white toilet paper. The plaster cast of Dollarhyde's teeth is white. Mann even takes this to another level when twice, people suspected of being the killer are revealed to be African-American and they are immediately discarded because – get this – they are not white! Mann seems to be saying that we may try to paint our world white, but we will never be able to paint over people like Lecter and Dollarhyde.

Shooting And Cutting: In a sly indictment of our own voyeuristic tendencies, *Manhunter* opens with the killer's point of view. But Mann is not, the way so many other inferior horror films do, encouraging us to get vicarious enjoyment out of what we are seeing. Rather, he is effectively setting up the primary conflict of the film. This is the killer's point of view, yes, but it is also Graham's point of view and if we need any proof that we are not to enjoy that view, we only need look at Graham himself and how tortured he is by this ability to see as the killer does. It's an almost telepathic sense of cinematic construction that informs every shot and cut. In the staging, for instance, Mann has Graham look at – and often talk to – his own reflection. In the airport as he leaves his family to be alone so that he can catch the killer, he tells his reflection in the window, "Just you and me now, Sport." We know he's figuratively talking to the killer but he is also looking straight into his own eyes. This is picked up on again when Graham deduces that the killer has seen the home movies of his victims. As Crawford discovers that Graham is right, Graham reaches out and grabs his own reflection in the glass. He has caught the killer because he has caught himself. As Graham and Crawford have their discussion on the beach about him coming back to work, Mann frames Crawford directly between Graham and his family, a unique underscore to the subtext of the scene. In the scene where Graham visits Lecter in his cell, Mann shoots it so that Lecter and Graham inhabit the frame in an identical way – they both seem to be behind bars. Through skillful editing, their faces, in effect, begin to become one another. Mann's camera often frames Graham so that he is cut off, a neat comment on the state of his character. And when Molly is alone in the house with Kevin, when we think Dollar-hyde may be outside, Mann's camera snakes past an aquarium because Molly is, thanks to Graham, living in a fishbowl, trapped and on display to the whole world.

Music: Mann did not ask Tangerine Dream back to score this, his third theatrical feature, instead opting to build his score from a combi-nation of custom music by electronic composers The Reds and Michel Rubini and existing material by such artists as Kitaro and former Tan-gerine Dream member Klaus Schulze. The result is no less effective, again not giving us Mann's personal taste but creating a reflection of the characters and story. As he hadn't done yet in one of his own movies, Mann also employed pop songs in a fashion similar to *Miami Vice* and *Crime Story*. The use of Iron Butterfly's 'In-A-Gadda-Da-Vida' over the final shoot-out is brilliant commentary not only on the twisted spiri-tual nature of Dollarhyde's 'becoming' but also on the bad acid-trip quality of his disturbed psyche. Urban legend has it that the song's title sprang from singer Doug Ingle's inability to say "in the Garden of Eden" because he was so high on LSD.

The Final Word: With all the quiet, terrifying grace of a black widow spider, *Manhunter* creeps onto screen, then works its way slowly into your brain. Thanks to the incredible performances and a script that doesn't permit any easy outs, this isn't a movie you'll soon forget. It's appropriate that we, the audience – like Will Graham in the film – are unable to wash the horrifying images we've seen from our brains. Given Mann's success at the time with both *Miami Vice* and *Crime Story*, producer Dino De Laurentiis must have been wondering what happened to his box office. But as we've seen three times already, Mann doesn't make easy movies. His films aren't the kind you grab a date, a soda and a bucket of popcorn to sit down with and watch. His movies get under your skin. And in the case of *Manhunter*, he gets into your head. This may be a film you'll want to think twice about watching, a look at police work that is as fascinating and enthralling as *Thief*'s look at crooks. And with the attention given to the character of Hannibal Lecter because of the success of both *The Silence Of The Lambs* and *Hannibal*, *Manhunter* has finally gotten the attention it went so long without. Many have pointed to Brian Cox's performance as much more chilling and effective than Anthony Hopkins' Oscar-winning turn and *Entertainment Weekly* even went so far as to call *Manhunter* "superior" to its sequel. They're right. And don't listen to the reviewers who decry the quality of the 'Director's Cut' disc in the limited edition DVD – it's worth every penny. Position on the Mann Top Ten List: #3.

NB: Although *Manhunter* and *The Silence Of The Lambs* share some of the same characters, only two actors appeared in both movies: Dan Butler and Frankie Faison. Both actors played different roles in each film. Actor Brian Cox and director Michael Mann both turned down the opportunity to make *The Silence Of The Lambs*: Cox refused because he "didn't do sequels" and Mann refused because he thought it was "heavy-duty." *Manhunter* is on the 'favorite films' list of Robert Englund, the actor better known as Freddy Krueger. The shot of Graham entering the Leeds' bedroom for the first time is the same angle and composition as Woermann's entrance into *The Keep*.

7. I Will Return

Sometime in 1948, when he was five years old, Mann visited a church in his neighborhood that showed movies in their basement to watch a 16mm print of the 1936 version of *The Last Of The Mohicans*. He would later recall this as the first film that made an impression on him. Unable then to identify what precisely so fascinated him about the movie, he later came to understand that it was the unique presentation of three different cultures, all joined together in what was effectively a war movie. When research of events in 1757 revealed a cultural backdrop very similar in a sense to Mann's own personal experience in the radical late 1960s, he began to see a way to retell the story, in spite of the fact that the source novel had already been filmed six times before – twice for television and four times as a theatrical feature. And that's just the American versions! On his own, Mann quickly acquired the rights to Philip Dunne's 1936 screenplay and wrote an outline detailing his new take on the material. When he walked into Joe Roth's and Roger Birnbaum's offices and told them, "I want to make *The Last Of The Mohicans* and I want to do it in a vivid, realistic way," they said, "Great idea!"

The Last Of The Mohicans (1992)

Directed by Michael Mann. Screenplay by Michael Mann and Christopher Crowe, based on the novel by James Fenimore Cooper and the 1936 screenplay by Philip Dunne.

The Cast: Daniel Day-Lewis (Hawkeye), Madeline Stowe (Cora Munro), Russell Means (Chingachgook), Eric Schweig (Uncas), Jodhi May (Alice Munro), Wes Studi (Magua), Steven Waddington (Heyward), Mac Andrews (General Webb), Maurice Roeves (Colonel Munro), Patrice Chereau (Montcalm), Pete Postlethwaite (Captain Beams), Colm Meaney (Major Ambrose)

The Crew: Produced by Hunt Lowry and Michael Mann. Music by Randy Edelman, Trevor Jones and Daniel Lanois. Photographed by Dante Spinotti. Edited by Dov Hoenig and Arthur Schmidt. Production Designed by Wolf Kroeger. Technical Advisor Dale Dye. 114 minutes. Director's Cut runs 117 minutes.

The Coverage: Titles tell us this is the year 1757, the third year of war between France and England for control of the American colonies. Three men are on the frontier west of the Hudson River. They are a Mohawk named Chingachgook, father to Uncas and adoptive father of Hawkeye. They pursue a deer and Hawkeye kills it with a single shot from his musket. They apologize to the deer for killing it and then thank it for providing them with food. That night, they arrive at the homestead of John Cameron and his family. Cameron is weighing a decision to join the Colonial Militia the British are trying to raise to fight the French. The next day, a British officer named Heyward works to muster the troops. Later, at a meeting with his superior officer, Heyward is told that he will be fighting at Fort William Henry under Colonel Munro. And he will be taking Munro's two daughters – Alice and Cora – with him. Magua, an Indian sent by Munro, will show them the way. Heyward then goes to see Cora Munro. Heyward again presses her to promise herself in marriage to him. She is evasive about the prospect. As Magua escorts Heyward, the Munro daughters and a group of soldiers to Fort William Henry, Hawkeye, along with Chingachgook and Uncas, track a war party through the forest. Suddenly Magua ambushes Munro and his men and the war party leaps from the trees to aid him in his slaughter of the soldiers. Hawkeye then emerges from the trees and battles the war party. Before Magua can kill Munro's daughters and Heyward, Hawkeye sends him running. Hawkeye, Chingachgook and Uncas then promise to take Heyward and the Munro daughters to Fort William Henry. Along the way, they pass by the Cameron homestead and find it completely burned. Everyone is dead and nothing has been taken. Clearly, this was not the work of robbers or bandits, but of a war party bent on destruction. Setting up camp for the night, Cora talks to Hawkeye, explaining that this wasn't what she expected when she came to the frontier to meet her father. They soon arrive at Fort William Henry and Hawkeye, Chingachgook and Uncas get Heyward and the Munro daughters past the marauding French soldiers to safety. Their father, Colonel Munro, is very upset. The situation at the fort is grave. The French troops advance at a speed that will spell defeat within three days. Munro wonders why his daughters didn't heed his letter and stay away. They say there was no such letter. Colonel Munro also asks where his reinforcement troops are and Heyward says they received no such request. When Munro explains that he sent three couriers, Heyward tells him the only courier who made it was Magua – the one who ambushed them. Colonel Munro now learns, however, that General Webb is at Fort Edward just twelve miles away. That may be close enough to secure reinforcements before the French get close enough to launch their final attack. Hawkeye now steps forward and tells Munro about the Cameron homestead. He says Webb promised that all members of the Colonial militia would be granted leave to defend their homes if any such attacks occurred. Munro says he cannot allow the men to leave based on the testimony of what one man saw at one location. Meanwhile, at the French camp, Magua meets with the French General, Montcalm, and tells him about what happened with Heyward and the daughters of Munro, who he calls 'Grey Hair'. Together, Montcalm and Magua plan their attack on Fort William Henry. Back inside the fort, Hawkeye and Cora begin to openly acknowledge their attraction to each other just before Hawkeye takes a position to cover the courier Munro has dispatched to Fort Edward to request reinforcements from General Webb. The courier makes it, thanks to Hawkeye's sharpshooting skills. Hawkeye then meets with Munro again and tries to explain to him what the situation is on the frontier and that he must allow the members of his Colonial Militia to leave the fort to defend their homes. Munro will not and again says that Hawkeye's proof is not enough. Hawkeye tries to get Heyward to back him up on his story, but Heyward lies, saying that he believes as Munro does, that it was an isolated incident. Munro tells Hawkeye that any man leaving the fort will be shot for desertion. Heyward then goes to see Cora and tells her that once they are back in England and married, none of this will matter. Cora at last tells Heyward that she will never marry him and he leaves. Meanwhile, Hawkeye talks to the members of the Militia. He will help them escape the fort so that they can defend their homes. Even though the rest of the men want him to come with them, he says he will stay behind. They guess that his reason wears a skirt and he tells them they are right. That night, Hawkeye and Cora at last give open expression to their blossoming love. Later, Hawkeye is roused in the middle of the night and arrested for his role in aiding the members of the Colonial Militia in leaving the fort. Cora immediately argues with her father about Hawkeye's arrest. But Colonel Munro holds fast. Cora goes to see Hawkeye in jail. He tells her that if the fort falls to the French, which it almost certainly will, she must stick close to her father so that he will be able to find her. As Hawkeye predicted, the French launch their final assault, inflicting heavy losses. The next morning, Montcalm and Munro meet outside the fort. Montcalm offers generous terms of surrender: he will allow Munro and his men to leave the fort fully armed if they promise to return to England and never come back. At first, Munro is reluctant. But when Montcalm hands over a message they intercepted from General Webb saying that no reinforcements can be spared, Munro accepts Montcalm's terms. That night, Magua tells Montcalm that he is very upset about the terms of surrender. He wanted to destroy the 'Grey Hair' because it was British troops who wiped out his whole family – including his children. Montcalm tells Magua that he must honor the terms of his surrender but that Magua is a man of his own will. The next morning, Munro leads his surviving troops out of the fort and as they begin the trek back to Albany, Magua and a giant war party emerge from the woods and begin slaughtering everyone. Hawkeye, Chingachgook, Uncas, Heyward, Alice and Cora all manage to escape with their lives. But Magua is in hot pursuit. As they hide out in a cave behind a giant waterfall, Hawkeye tells Cora that he must leave her behind because it's their only hope for survival. He says he will find her and then departs. Magua and his men find the cave and capture Heyward, Alice and Cora. As they march them through the woods, Hawkeye tracks them. Magua arrives at a Huron camp and seeks acknowledgement from Sachem, the leader. He shows them his valuable prisoners. Just then, however, Hawkeye enters and although they first try to stop him, he is at last allowed to present his own case to Sachem. He tells the Huron leader that Magua is a liar. At last, Sachem says that Alice can go with Magua, that Heyward can be allowed to return to his superior officers and that Cora will burn for what the "Greyhair" did to Magua's children. Hawkeye tells Sachem to take him instead of Cora, but Heyward convinces the Indian to take him instead. Hawkeye and Cora quickly flee while Heyward is burned alive. Meanwhile, Magua takes Alice with him to find Huron leaders who will listen to him. Hawkeye, Chingachgook, Uncas and Cora now pursue Magua and Alice. They catch up to them on the trail, Uncas first. During hand-to-hand combat, Magua kills Uncas. Alice then throws herself off the cliff and at last, Chingachgook confronts and kills Magua. Alone at the edge of the frontier, Hawkeye, Chingachgook and Cora contemplate what their future holds.

Research: Mann did not want to bring 1757 into the 1990s. Instead, he wanted to take what historians had come to understand through the 1990s and imprint it back onto 1757. In other words, he wanted to use the contemporary perspective as a tool to construct a more intense experience of realistic people in a complex time. He also researched actual accounts of the battles depicted, in the form of diaries written by soldiers who had fought there. For visual inspiration, Mann looked at N C Wyeth's paintings for the Scribner's Classics edition of *The Last Of The Mohicans*, but he really wanted to see how artists saw the environment of the time and since it no longer existed by the time Wyeth was working, he concentrated instead on looking at nineteenth-century landscape painters such as Thomas Cole and Albert Bierstadt. Also, as he had done with James Caan on *Thief* and William Petersen on *Manhunter*, Mann put his actors through training with a technical advisor. Starting with contemporary weapons and working their way back to black powder, Daniel Day-Lewis reportedly became a crack shot and, after only a day and a half, was able to knock everything down with a .45. The result is a group of performances with attitude that can't be performed.

Story: The so-called 'dangerous deals' we have come to expect in the films of Michael Mann are here for the first time pushed to the sidelines while a different kind of deal is brought center stage. Thus, the deals between the British generals and the Colonial Militia, and between Magua and Montcalm fit the typical Mann scenario. That is, the attachments formed result in destruction. Magua dies as a direct result of his deal with Montcalm. Had he not undertaken the massacre of the British after they surrendered Fort William Henry, Hawkeye, Chingachgook and Uncas would have had no reason to hunt him down and kill him. Similarly, the members of the Colonial Militia lose their entire families because of their binding deal with the British. But Hawkeye is our protagonist and although he risks his life to help Cora, there is neither the same sense of danger in nor the same result as the other deals. Like Graham, Hawkeye must honor his obligation in order to become complete. Unlike Graham, however, the completion of his obligation actually makes things better for him. Cora's family has been completely wiped out, it's true, but she has Hawkeye. And Hawkeye's brother has been killed, yes, but he has Cora. All this makes Hawkeye the weakest example of a Mann Man.

The Mann Man: True, he is dedicated to what he does and he does undertake a dangerous deal, but his epiphany comes without the cost associated with characters such as Frank or Graham. Unlike the other Mann Men, Hawkeye is motivated purely by love. And his dreams of love, connection and domesticity are never deceptive attachments but are rather real things that he can both get his hands on and get real meaning out of. It's the first Mann movie that ends with the protagonist together with a woman in the most normal sense. And in spite of Chingachgook's closing speech lamenting the loss of the frontier, there is little sense of personal sacrifice at the end. How can there be? Hawkeye and Cora have each other and this, we are led to believe, is enough.

Design: Mann's goal with *The Last Of The Mohicans* was similar to *The Jericho Mile* in the sense that he wanted it to be, above all else, realistic. As he had discovered on *The Keep*, however, almost every-thing he required didn't exist anymore, so they made it all – from the clothing of six different Indian tribes to the construction of all the weapons. This level of detail reaches into even the unseen corners of the film. To construct Fort William Henry, for instance, nails were used that were exact replicas of the period! The end result, while attaining an authenticity that approaches documentary realism, also lacks much of the kind of "tricky visual language" Mann has so effectively deployed in almost every other film.

Shooting And Cutting: From the start, it was clear to Mann that he could not shoot this movie in the same way that he had *Manhunter*. This was supposed to be 1757, after all, so the lighting had to be approached, like everything else, realistically. Having once visited a restored home in Wisconsin in which the owners had restored even the gas fixtures, Mann knew what he was looking for. Working together with his cam-eraman, Dante Spinotti, they developed what would form the two prin-cipal light sources for the movie: the orange-red glow associated with firelight and the silver-blue associated with moonlight. This presented a particular challenge for the Fort William Henry set, which had been constructed full-size, on location – about 40 acres. Bringing in cranes over 200 feet high, they then suspended lights called 'dinos' from these cranes. Each about the size of a billboard with many small lamps mak-ing up the total light source, these lights were positioned over the huge set just out of camera range, providing both the proper look and enough light to expose the film properly.

Music: For the first time, Mann used something that approached a standard score by hiring Randy Edelman and Trevor Jones. As always, this was not based on personal taste, but again was a choice appropriate for the movie itself. In many instances, period instruments were used for the score, adding to the element of realism even on the soundtrack. Sharp ears take note: composer Trevor Jones reused some of the themes from *The Last Of The Mohicans* in his score for the Sylvester Stallone movie *Cliffhanger*!

The Final Word: A standout in terms of its look and design, *The Last Of The Mohicans* is, unfortunately, thin when compared to the rest of Mann's work, marred by a Hollywood-style romance and an over-reliance on the kind of easy outs he has managed to avoid in every other film. In spite of these factors – perhaps more accurately because of these factors – it proved to be his most successful film in terms of domestic US box office, totaling just over $72 million. Even so, as *The Keep* had before it, *The Last Of The Mohicans* proved that Mann is not a film-maker limited by genre, he is instead a film artist who brings to each project his characteristic style and dedication. So although it stands as his second weakest effort (surpassed only by *L.A. Takedown*), *The Last Of The Mohicans* is still definitely a title to add to your Michael Mann collection – just not before much else. Position on the Mann Top Ten List: #9.

NB: *The Last Of The Mohicans* won the Academy Award for Best Achievement In Sound. For the Director's Cut of the movie, Mann cut five minutes and added eight minutes. He also removed popular Irish group Clannad from the soundtrack because he felt the music was too sentimental and was taking some of the emotional power away from the story.

8. L.A. Crime Sagas

Most film-makers, it would seem, have a dream project, the one script or story they often talk about but sometimes never get the opportunity to make. Ironically, Mann got to make his twice. Originally written in the 1970s, *Heat* was about a cop and a criminal, both dedicated professionals with mutual respect even though they are on opposite sides of the law. As they close in on each other, they even have the chance to sit down and discuss their similarities prior to the final duel in which the cop kills the crook. Mann knew the script was unique, unlike anything that had appeared before and he was determined to see it made. At last, in 1989, he had the chance to direct it as a TV movie. But with only ten days of pre-production and 19 days of shooting, the limited schedule and resources couldn't come close to doing the script any real justice. The title was changed to *L.A. Takedown* for broadcast.

Flash forward to 1992, when *The Last Of The Mohicans* scored so heavily on all fronts and Mann saw the opportunity to return to the original version of the script. Armed this time with a budget of $60 million, Mann was able to attract both Robert De Niro and Al Pacino – a real casting coup for this type of movie. His budget also bought him a six-month pre-production period and a 107-day shooting schedule.

Comparing both versions of the same story is, Mann once said, like "comparing freeze-dried coffee with Jamaican Blue Mountain." Nothing could be truer. Whereas *L.A. Takedown* is the only film that doesn't feel like it's got all of Mann's energy behind it, *Heat* seems to have 200% of him. And what's especially interesting is the unique opportunity to see a film-maker remaking his own material. Mann once said that he believed all directors want to revisit their own films, to tinker and rework them until they are perfect. And while he's had the opportunity to edit 'Director's Cuts' of three of his movies (*Thief*, *Manhunter* and *The Last Of The Mohicans*), not since Alfred Hitchcock has a film-maker had the opportunity to make two films from the same script – and never within six years of each other! Viewing the two back to back is a film student's dream for at last you can see and hear how design, direction, performance and post-production all result in dramatically different effects. In this case, the second time was the charm with *Heat* being the fullest expression of Mann's 'street picture' side.

L.A. Takedown (1989)

Written and Directed by Michael Mann.

The Cast: Scott Plank (Vincent Hanna), Alex McArthur (Patrick McClaren), Michael Rooker (Bosko), Ely Pouget (Lillian), Richard Chaves (Casals), Victor Rivers (Arriaga), Peter Dobson (Chris Shiherlis), Robert Winley (Nate), Vincent Guastaferro (Michael Ceritto), Laura Harrington (Eady), Jentry Tuvil (Charlene Shiherlis), Cary-Hiroyuki Tagawa (Hugh Denny), Donald Grant (Dr Bob), Juan Fernandez (Harvey Torena), Xander Berkeley (Waingro)

The Crew: Produced by Michael Mann and Patrick Markey. Music by Tim Truman. Photographed by Ron Garcia. Edited by Dov Hoenig. Production Designed by Dean Taucher. 92 minutes. Aka *L.A. Crimewave* and *Made In L.A.*

The Coverage: At home, police detective Vincent Hanna wakes up and heads into the shower. His wife joins him and they make love before he goes to work. Meanwhile, Ceritto and Waingro, two members of an expert crew of thieves led by Patrick McClaren, get ready to rob an armored car. Waingro is clearly not a professional. He talks so much Ceritto has to tell him to shut up. The crew dons hockey masks and rams the armored car with a garbage truck, turning it over. Quickly, the crew blows the doors of the armored car and pulls out the guards. Just as they get what they were looking for – bearer bonds – Waingro loses his cool and shoots one of the guards. A skirmish breaks out and when Ceritto's hockey mask is removed, the gang kills all the guards. Ceritto tells Waingro, "You blew it, Sport," and the gang flees the scene. Vincent gets a call about the robbery and promptly pays a visit to an informant named Torena. Next visiting the crime scene, Vincent tells his fellow officers that these guys are good. Meanwhile, Patrick and his crew meet with Waingro in a restaurant. Patrick tells them he wants to pay Waingro off and get rid of him. As they leave, Patrick tries to kill Waingro, but when a passing police car distracts him, Waingro escapes. On the street, Vincent interviews other informants, then heads to the bar where his wife works. Just as they are talking about having a nice evening together, Vincent is called away and must visit Torena again. Before he can barely get the investigation into the armored car robbery underway, Vincent gets another call about a new crime. This time, he arrives on the scene of the murder of a young prostitute. Vincent heads home at last and he and his wife talk about just how hard his job is. Meanwhile, in a sleazy hotel room, Waingro prepares to kill another prostitute. At a restaurant, Eady, a regular working woman, strikes up a conversation with Patrick. He is defensive at first, but then apologizes and continues talking to her. They go to her house and make love. When Vincent's wife wakes up the next morning, he is already gone. Vincent meets Torena again and his friend explains that he met an ex-con on the street who he is sure had something to do with the armored car heist. Vincent doesn't buy it until Torena's friend says, "This Sport is for real." Vincent now knows this is the guy and he finds out his name is Ceritto. At dinner with his whole crew and their wives, Patrick explains that this next score is going to be his last. Then, jealous of the relationships his friends have, he calls Eady and tells her he wants to see her again. Outside the restaurant, Vincent watches as Patrick's gang exits. Vincent plans to keep watch on all of them so that whatever they put down next, they can catch them in the act. Later that night, the cops party at the bar owned by Vincent's wife. When one of her employees comes onto her, Vincent beats him up, upsetting his wife. Vincent explains that the job takes its toll, but she doesn't want anything more to do with him. Patrick asks Eady to go away with him and she agrees. Patrick then meets with his crew and finds out that they have all been made – their cars and phones are bugged. Patrick wants to go through with their last job anyway and he tells each of them that they have to decide on their own if they want to as well. Everyone agrees. Next, Patrick takes his crew to an open area and acts like they are casing a job. As soon as they leave, Vincent and the police head down to try and see what Patrick was looking at. Only too late, Vincent realizes that Patrick is now looking at them – that they've been made. Patrick talks to Nate about Vincent. Nate explains that he's a real go-getter and that although he has made the rest of the crew, he hasn't yet made Patrick. Meanwhile, Waingro tries to find other work as a criminal. The next day, as

Vincent stops to pick up laundry, he spots Patrick in the parking lot. And Patrick spots him. In a bold move, Vincent invites Patrick to have a cup of coffee with him and Patrick accepts. At a nearby restaurant, the two men discuss each other and find that they have a lot in common. Patrick says that he will not stop doing what he is doing. And Vincent says the same thing to Patrick. They leave and when Vincent returns to the office, he is told by his fellow officers that Patrick and his crew dumped all their surveillance at the same time. Vincent can hardly believe it. How could something like that happen? Just then, Patrick and his crew conduct the first part of their bank job. At a restaurant, Patrick's driver backs out of the job, claiming that he can't get away. No sooner has he left than he goes to meet with Waingro who wants to know if Patrick bought it. He assures him he did. Patrick and his crew now enter the bank and begin the robbery. Just then, Vincent is tipped off that Patrick's crew is performing a bank heist at that very moment. Vincent and the police hurry to the bank and as Patrick and the others come out, a shoot-out begins. Chris is shot but Patrick manages to escape by hijacking a car at a nearby supermarket. Ceritto escapes a different way and when he tries to use a little girl to get away from the police, Vincent shoots him dead. Vincent wants to know who ratted Patrick out. Patrick takes Chris to see Dr Bob for his gunshot wound, threatening the doctor to keep quiet about it. Vincent goes to see Hugh Denny and finds out that Waingro was the insider. Meanwhile, Patrick goes to see his driver and discovers him left for dead. He apologizes to Patrick but explains that they had Anna, his wife, and there was nothing he could do. Patrick wants to know who it was and he says, "Waingro." Vincent finds out where Waingro is and orders the word put on the street, hoping that Patrick will be unable to leave without settling his score with Waingro. Patrick now finds out from Nate that a plane will be waiting for him at the airport. Patrick wants Nate to find out where Waingro is, then he goes to see Eady. She can't believe Patrick is responsible for the bank robbery she saw on the news. She runs from him but he tells her that his criminal life is over and he wants her to come with him. She reluctantly agrees. Meanwhile, Vincent and the police stake out Waingro at his hotel, but they think Patrick must be gone by now. Vincent goes to the hospital and makes up with his wife.

x

Patrick tries to convince Eady to come with him one last time, but she can't. Patrick talks to Nate and finds out where Waingro is. He heads to the hotel and when he shows up, the stake-out crew quickly lets Vincent know. As Patrick lures Waingro to the door so he can kill him, Vincent arrives on the scene. Distracted, Patrick is shot by Waingro and dies in Vincent's arms. Vincent then kills Waingro by pushing him out of the window. As he leaves the hotel, Vincent meets his wife.

Heat (1995)

Written and Directed by Michael Mann.

The Cast: Al Pacino (Vincent Hanna), Robert De Niro (Neil McCauley), Val Kilmer (Chris Shiherlis), Jon Voight (Nate), Tom Sizemore (Michael Cheritto), Diane Venora (Justine Hanna), Amy Brenneman (Eady), Ashley Judd (Charlene Shiherlis), Mykelti Williamson (Drucker), Wes Studi (Casals), Natalie Portman (Lauren), Tom Noonan (Kelso), Kevin Gage (Waingro), Hank Azaria (Marciano), Danny Trejo (Trejo), Henry Rollins (Hugh Benny), Tone Loc (Richard Torena), Jeremy Piven (Dr Bob), Xander Berkeley (Ralph), Bud Cort (Restaurant Manager)

The Crew: Produced by Art Linson and Michael Mann. Music by Elliot Goldenthal, Brian Eno, Terje Rypdal and Kronos Quartet. Photographed by Dante Spinotti. Edited by Pasquale Buba, William Goldenberg, Dov Hoenig and Tom Rolf. Production Designed by Neil Spisak. Technical Advisor Chuck Adamson. 171 minutes.

The Coverage: A train pulls into a station and Neil McCauley gets off. Dressed in a paramedic's uniform, he walks into a nearby hospital and drives off with an ambulance. Somewhere in Arizona, Chris Shiherlis buys a crate of explosives. At home in Los Angeles, police detective Vincent Hanna wakes up and makes love with his wife. He then heads into the shower. She asks him to stay for coffee, but he says he is out of time and has to get going. Meanwhile, his wife's daughter, Lauren, enters, anxious about the impending arrival of her father. Vincent doubts the guy will show up and he leaves. Lauren demands her mother pay attention to her. At a restaurant, Waingro is picked up in a giant tow truck driven by Michael Cheritto. Waingro is clearly not a professional.

He talks so much Cheritto has to tell him to shut up. The crew dons hockey masks and rams an armored car with the tow truck, turning it over. Quickly, the crew blows the doors of the armored car and pulls out the guards. Just as they get what they were looking for – bearer bonds – Waingro starts to lose his cool. Cheritto tells him, "Cool it, Slick." But Waingro can't and when he shoots one of the guards, a brief shoot-out ensues in which Neil and his gang kill the rest of the guards. The gang then flees the scene. Neil meets with Nate to collect the money for the stolen bearer bonds. Nate wonders if they shouldn't try to sell them back to their owner, Roger Van Zant. Neil tells him to try it out. Also, Nate tells him that Kelso has a big bank job planned and he thinks Neil should have a look at it. Neil agrees and leaves. Vincent arrives at the crime scene and tells his fellow officers that this crew is good. Meanwhile, Neil and his crew meet with Waingro in a restaurant. Neil tells them he wants to pay Waingro off and get rid of him. As they leave, Neil actually tries to kill Waingro, but when a passing police car distracts him, Waingro escapes. Neil goes home alone. Chris goes home to Charlene and they argue about their money problems. Chris leaves. Vincent goes home to Justine and they argue. At a restaurant, Eady, a bookstore clerk, strikes up a conversation with Neil. He is defensive at first, but then apologizes and continues talking to her. They go to Neil's house and make love. Vincent pays a visit to an informant named Torena. Torena promises he will have information for him via his brother the next night. Neil meets Kelso about the bank job and agrees to take it on. Then Nate tells Neil that he talked to Van Zant and that he wants to play. Neil should call him to make the collection. Neil goes home and finds Chris asleep on his floor. They talk about his problems with Charlene. Meanwhile, Breedan, a parolee, says goodbye to his girlfriend as he reports for his first day on a legitimate job. When he enters the restaurant, the manager tells him how part of his pay kicks back to him and that if he doesn't play along, he'll violate him back to jail. Neil calls Van Zant and arranges for the pay-off at a drive-in theater. At the same time, Neil sees Alan Marciano leaving Charlene in a hotel room. Neil goes in and tells Charlene she will give Chris one last chance and that she is to go home. Vincent now meets the Torena brothers at a bar. Richard Torena explains that he met an ex-con on the street he is sure had something to do with the armored car heist. Vincent doesn't buy it until Torena says, "This Slick is for real." Vincent knows this is the guy and he finds out his name is Cheritto. At the abandoned drive-in, Neil waits to pick up the money from Van Zant. When Van Zant's men try to kill Neil, his crew promptly kills Van Zant's assassins. Neil calls Van Zant and tells him to forget about the money, he is a dead man. At dinner with his whole crew and their wives, Neil gets jealous of the relationships his friends have, so he calls Eady to tell her he wants to see her again. Outside the restaurant, Vincent watches as Neil's gang exits. Vincent plans to keep watch on all of them so that whatever they put down next, they can catch them in the act. Meanwhile, in a sleazy hotel room, Waingro prepares to kill a prostitute. Afterwards, Waingro visits a bar to find other work as a criminal. Later that night, the cops party at a restaurant. In the middle of dancing with his wife, Vincent gets a page and leaves. This time, he arrives on the scene of the murder of the young prostitute that Waingro killed. When he returns to the restaurant hours later, Justine is still waiting for him. They talk about just how hard his job is. Vincent explains that the job takes its toll, but she doesn't want anything more to do with him. Breedan tells his girlfriend about what happened on the job, but he promises he will try to stick to it. Eady and Neil continue to develop their relationship. Then Vincent spots Lauren on the street and takes her home. At a stake-out, Vincent watches as Neil and his crew go to work robbing a precious metals storage facility. But when a rookie cop tips Neil to their presence, they walk away. Vincent has to let them go. Neil meets with his crew and tells them they have to assume that the police have everything. Neil wants to go through with the bank job anyway and he tells each of them that they have to decide on their own if they want to as well. Everyone agrees. Vincent now pays a visit to Alan Marciano and tells him that he will be working for them now, helping them get to Neil and his crew through his relationship with Charlene. Next, Neil takes his crew to an open area and acts like they are casing a job. As soon as they leave, Vincent and the police head down to try and see what Neil was looking at. Only too late, Vincent realizes that Neil is now looking at them – that they've been made. Neil talks to Nate about Vincent. Nate explains that he's a real go-getter and that although he has made the rest of the crew, he hasn't yet made Neil. Vincent arrives home and finds Justine ready to go out without him. He leaves and pulls Neil over on the freeway. In a bold move, Vincent invites Neil to have a cup of coffee with him and Neil accepts. At a nearby restaurant, the two men discuss each other and find that they have a lot in common. Neil says that he will not stop doing what he is doing. And Vincent says the same thing to Neil. When Vincent returns to the office, he is told by his fellow officers that Neil and his crew dumped all their surveillance at the same time. Vincent can hardly believe it. How could something like that happen? Just then, Neil and his crew conduct the first part of their bank job, cutting into the alarm system computer. Then Van Zant, who has been living in his office because he's too afraid to go out, meets Waingro. Waingro says he can help Van Zant get Neil. At a restaurant, Trejo, Neil's driver, backs out of the job, claiming he can't get away from the police. Neil then spots Breedan, who he recognizes from prison. Needing a driver, he quickly invites him along. With Eady at home packing and Charlene at home with her son, Neil and his crew now enter the bank and begin the robbery. Just then, Vincent is tipped off that Neil's crew is perform-ing a bank heist at that very moment. Vincent and the police hurry to the bank and as Neil and the others come out, a shoot-out begins. Chris is shot but Neil manages to escape by hijacking a car at a nearby super-market. Cheritto escapes a different way and when he tries to use a little girl as a hostage, Vincent shoots him dead. Breedan's girlfriend now sees the story on the news about his death during the bank job. Neil takes Chris to see Dr Bob for his gunshot wound, threatening the doctor to keep quiet about it. He tells Chris that Nate will come to pick him up. But Chris won't leave without Charlene. When Charlene sees what hap-pened on the news, she calls Alan Marciano and the police jump on the chance to catch Chris. Meanwhile, Neil goes to see Trejo and discovers him left for dead. Trejo apologizes to Neil but explains that they had Anna, his wife, and there was nothing he could do. Neil wants to know who it was and Trejo tells him it was Waingro, who is now working for Van Zant. Trejo begs Neil to kill him and he does so. Neil calls Nate and tells him that he needs a new escape method and he needs to know where Waingro is. Neil then visits Van Zant and kills him. Vincent goes to see Hugh Benny and finds out that Waingro was the insider. He also

71

finds out where Waingro is and orders the word put on the street. He hopes that Neil will be unable to leave without settling his score with Waingro. Marciano now takes Charlene to his place where the police are waiting. They tell her that this is her chance to get out from under Chris and do something for Dominic, her son. She agrees. Neil goes to see Eady. She can't believe Neil is the guy responsible for the bank robbery she saw on the news. She runs from him but he tells her that his criminal life is over and he wants her to come with him. Later, Neil finds out from Nate what his new escape method is. Neil also finds out that Chris is gone. Neil tries to convince Eady to come with him one last time, and she finally agrees. Chris arrives at the house to get Charlene, but she signals him to keep moving. He drives away. Vincent leaves the office, convinced that Neil is gone. He arrives at his hotel and finds Lauren in the bathtub, nearly dead from a suicide attempt. He quickly takes her to the hospital where he meets Justine and comforts her. Neil is on his way out when Nate calls to tell him where Waingro is. Neil decides he can't leave unfinished business and so he drives to the hotel and leaves Eady in the car. Inside the hotel, he pulls fire alarm, then goes to get Waingro. Back at the hospital, Vincent tells Justine that he isn't what she wants and when he gets a page, he leaves to go to the hotel. Inside, Neil kills Waingro and avoids being captured by the police. But when he gets downstairs and is getting back in his car with Eady, he spots Vincent closing in and he takes off running. Vincent hunts down Neil through the maze of the nearby airport and at last shoots him dead.

Research: Chuck Adamson, the Chicago police officer who was one of the technical advisors on *Thief* and who later created *Crime Story*, is the one who told Mann this story originally, having hunted down and killed the real Neil McCauley in Chicago in 1963. With this as the central focus, Mann then also drew inspiration for the character of Vincent Hanna from a friend of his who runs large operations against drug cartels in foreign countries. Further expanding his research of the mindset of cops and crooks, he also interviewed other members of law enforcement and discovered that they are not emotionally incomplete, but rather that they thrive on the visceral high of hunting. Similarly, in talking with ex-convicts, he found out that they are rarely total sociopaths.

One such individual told Mann that even someone serving a life sentence in Folsom wakes up once every two months in the middle of the night and asks themselves, "How did I screw up my life this bad?" Again putting his performers through the same routine, Mann had Ashley Judd talk to women who were married to convicts or ex-convicts. And while some of them told stories about turning twenty tricks a night when they were 17 years old, others were middle-aged, intelligent and well dressed. In addition to training with an expert in urban warfare, De Niro spent time with thieves and convicts and went very deeply into their emotions. As always, the result is a cluster of performances containing an attitude that can't be acted.

Story: With a scope even more sprawling than *The Last Of The Mohicans* (and, for that matter, even *L.A. Takedown*), *Heat* tells a story about the connections between everyone. Like some sort of Chinese puzzle, the film progressively reveals layer after layer of connections and (of course) dangerous deals: Neil and Nate, Nate and Kelso, Nate and Van Zant, Kelso and Neil, Waingro and Van Zant, Charlene and Marciano, Marciano and Vincent, Vincent and Torena, Torena and Cheritto, Neil and Eady. This isn't just an action movie, this is a sociological examination of what happens when people live and work together. Everyone has their own agenda. Everyone has their own reasons for doing what they do. These are the things that reside in everyone's heart, unknown and beyond the control of anyone else, which is precisely what makes them so perilous. The only way to survive in this environment is to use the connections without letting them use you (as Vincent does) or to have no connection you cannot walk out on in thirty seconds (as Neil does). This makes both Vincent and Neil interesting versions of the Mann Man.

The Mann Man: While all of Mann's protagonists share a unique kinship with one another, Vincent and Neil are unique in that they literally seem to have been transposed from two previous films and combined in one story. Neil is a veritable transcription of Frank from *Thief*. Both men learned their philosophies from father figures while in prison. Both men know the way to survive is to have no connections. And both men succumb to forming attachments outside of themselves in an attempt to give their lives meaning. Vincent, on the other hand, is a transcription of Graham from *Manhunter*. Both of these men know their dedication to what they do costs them their attachments. Both men very nearly become their prey in order to catch them. The difference, ultimately, is that while Frank manages to shed his connections before they completely destroy him, Neil is unable to do so. Once he has violated his philosophy and tries to maintain his attachments, he plummets into self-destruction. But the comment contained within this statement is less about the danger of the philosophy itself than it is about the results of the abandonment of one's personal beliefs. Thus Mann's philosophy remains unchanged: Vincent survives because he remains true to himself; Neil does not because he betrays himself. As it is and always shall be in Michael Mann's filmic world: the ultimate crime is not thievery or killing, but betrayal of self.

Design: Compared to *Heat*, both *Manhunter* and *Thief* seem positively over-designed, especially with their use of color and architecture as reflections of character and situation. Similar elements are present in *Heat*, but they are not as easily defined or identifiable. Instead, Mann opted for a more realistic approach, underscoring the story's realistic quality. So that while red may often indicate danger or death (in the scene where Waingro kills the prostitute, the hotel they occupy has red doors, she wears a red bra and panties and immediately following her murder, Waingro sits in a bar, framed against a red background) it can also serve as the color of the police (in the scene where Vincent sees Neil for the first time, he hides behind a giant red neon sign). Blue may have romantic overtones (Neil is framed against a blue background when he calls Eady to ask her out the second time) but it can also signify danger and death (Neil must step around a blue pool just before he kills Van Zant). All of this tells us that in real life, things can have more than one meaning, depending on your point of view. Similar to its use in both *The Keep* and *Manhunter*, architecture works to underscore the 'similar opposite' quality of Vincent and Neil. Thus Neil's house, in spite of the spectacular ocean view his wealth has afforded him, is like his life: cold (the color scheme all white and polished steel) and empty (literalized by its lack of furnishings). Vincent's house is very nearly the same, although he attributes it not to himself, but to his wife's ex-husband. When Vincent tells Ralph it's "dead-tech" and "postmodernist," his disdain is as clear as the fact that he might as well be referring to Neil's place. Neil may choose to live in such an environment, but Vincent lives here only because he chases guys like Neil. Other design elements worth looking for include the cap Breedan wears when Neil asks him to drive his getaway car – it's covered with dancing skeletons, a neat foreshadowing of his impending death. And in the moments before the police start shooting at Neil and Chris after the bank job, the vehicles that stand in their way are a moving truck and a bus displaying an ad for Thai Air, a neat comment on Neil's dream of moving to a foreign country by flying away. And like *Thief*, Mann's conscious attention to design again finds its way even into the structure of the film. In spite of *Heat* running 172 minutes and *L.A. Takedown* running only 92 minutes, both feature the exact same first 'turning point'. At exactly 30 minutes in, Neil and Eady kiss.

Shooting And Cutting: As with *Manhunter*, Mann sets up the primary conflict of the film with a purely visual statement. The opening pair of shots – first of a train (screen left) moving toward us through a tangle of wires and clouds of steam, then of the same train moving away from us (screen right) into utter blackness broken only by a cold neon blue sculpture – is the perfect metaphor for Neil and Vincent. For what are both men but trains, locked onto the tracks of the lives they have chosen for themselves, moving through a series of entanglements into the darkness of the heart of the city? And even though we know it's the same train, the change in screen position serves as a neat comment on the opposite similarity of both protagonists. It's the same telepathic sense of cinematic construction with which Mann informs every film. In the shot showing Neil descending the escalator in the train station, Mann uses such an extreme telephoto lens that Neil appears to be moving straight down, what he will literally do as the movie progresses. In the scene where Chris buys explosives, Mann frames the last shot in such a way that the warning sign replaces Chris' head. Won't his explosive nature prove to be his own downfall? When Waingro boards the tow truck with Cheritto, a Sega sign is visible through the window beyond them, neatly telling us that Waingro's 'videogame' attitude towards crime will unravel Neil's whole gang and his whole life. In the sequence where the police stake out the precious-metals facility while

75

Neil breaks in, Vincent employs a thermal camera which, on the black and white monitors Vincent uses to watch him, renders Neil's face in negative, another neat comment on how these men reflect each other. And in what must rank as one of the most brilliant instances of staging, Neil and Chris escape from the bank job by fleeing to a nearby supermarket, forcing Vincent to take cover behind a row of barbecues that Neil promptly destroys in a hail of machine-gun fire. In their conversation in the coffee shop, Vincent had asked Neil if he didn't ever want a regular life. Neil's response: "Like barbecues?" The very thing that now stands between them, destroyed by the gunfire that represents their real, irregular lives. As the scene ends, Neil and Chris escape in a station wagon full of groceries, another perfect emblem of a domestic life turned upside down.

Music: For *L.A. Takedown*, Mann used fairly straightforward rock and roll, including a pop song employed for effect. That track is Billy Idol's cover version of 'L.A. Woman' by The Doors. What more succinct comment could he make about Los Angeles than using a song about the city as woman updated by a performer nearly synonymous with the dark side of Hollywood glitz? For *Heat*, Mann combined Moby, Brian Eno, Kronos Quartet, William Orbit, Gyorgi Ligeti (whose music was used by Kubrick for both *2001* and *Eyes Wide Shut*), Terje Rypdal, Lisa Gerrard and a few custom cues by Eliot Goldenthal to create a soundtrack unlike anything that had been heard before – especially for something like an urban action picture. More proof that he refuses to be hampered by generic conventions and instead seeks out ways to best enhance the story.

The Final Word: While *L.A. Takedown* nearly disappeared into obscurity (it's been released on home video under several alternate titles), *Heat* burst onto the screen in a way no Michael Mann film had yet. Thanks in large part to the presence of Robert De Niro and Al Pacino, *Heat* was a major Hollywood release in every sense. Richard Schickel of *Time* magazine said it had "truly epic sweep, maniacal conviction and awesome technical proficiency." And while business was lukewarm in the US, with box office totaling only about $67 million, *Heat* ended up grossing over $187 million worldwide. Viewing both of these films together in the context of Mann's whole career is a rare opportunity to see the summation of everything he knows about action film-making. The end result is a unique pair of films. *Heat* is a classic of its kind, far surpassing what we've come to expect from a crime drama – even when compared to *Thief*. And *L.A. Takedown* is worth seeking out solely for the purpose of seeing just how much difference budget and schedule can make. Positions on the Mann Top Ten List: *L.A. Takedown*: #10, *Heat*: #2.

NB: *Heat* was particularly successful in France, selling 1.3 million admissions. Neil McCauley's line to Roger Van Zant, "I am talking to a dead man," was lifted from *The Jericho Mile*. It's what Dr D tells Murphy after he burns his cash. The direction of the TV version of the film is credited to Alan Smithee because Mann was upset with NBC's inept removal of 17 minutes. Xander Berkeley, who plays Ralph, appeared in *L.A. Takedown* as Waingro. Hank Azaria, who plays Alan Marciano, is also known as the voice of Apu, Moe and Police Chief Wiggums on *The Simpsons*. The location chosen for the bank really is a bank and has appeared in a number of other films, most notably as the Treasury Department headquarters in William Friedkin's *To Live And Die In L.A.* Technical Advisor Andy McNab was part of a special forces team used during the Gulf War to sabotage SCUD missile sites behind enemy lines. The Terje Rypdal composition 'Mystery Man' appears in both *L.A. Takedown* and *Heat*. The word that gives Cheritto away in *L.A. Takedown* is "Sport" (what Graham calls Dollarhyde in *Manhunter*) while the word that gives him away in *Heat* is "Slick" (what Attaglia calls Frank in *Thief*). When LAX air traffic disrupted production one night, the crew sent T-bone steaks to the controllers to get them to redirect the planes over the ocean until the shoot could be completed.

9. Oscar Calling

Michael Mann met *60 Minutes* producer Lowell Bergman through Bill Alden, a mutual friend in the DEA. When Bergman and Mann first met, they tried developing projects around stories Bergman had worked on, such as one involving arms merchants in Marbella. But in 1995, while Mann was in post-production on *Heat*, Bergman kept calling him to discuss the story he was then working on about a tobacco company whistle-blower named Jeffrey Wigand. Mann finally told Bergman to forget about everything else they had been discussing, what he was going through right then was a real story. Mann wasn't alone in his thinking. At the same time, investigative journalist Marie Brenner published her 20,000-word take on the events, 'The Man Who Knew Too Much', in *Vanity Fair*. And although Mann had an inside connection to the proceedings through Bergman, the Brenner article gave him what he didn't have: Jeffrey Wigand, the insider himself. Buying the rights to the piece, Mann and screenwriter Eric Roth took up residence in the Broadway Deli in Santa Monica and began work on the script that would result in Mann's most acclaimed movie to date.

The Insider (1999)

Directed by Michael Mann. Screenplay by Michael Mann and Eric Roth, from the article 'The Man Who Knew Too Much' by Marie Brenner, originally published in *Vanity Fair*.

The Cast: Al Pacino (Lowell Bergman), Russell Crowe (Jeffrey Wigand), Christopher Plummer (Mike Wallace), Diane Venora (Liane Wigand), Philip Baker Hall (Don Hewitt), Lindsay Crouse (Sharon Tiller), Debi Mazar (Debbie De Luca), Stephen Tobolowsky (Eric Kluster), Gina Gershon (Helen Caperelli), Rip Torn (John Scanlon), Wings Hauser (Tobacco Lawyer), Michael Moore (Himself)

The Crew: Produced by Michael Mann, Pieter Jan Brugge and Michael Waxman. Music by Pieter Bourke, Lisa Gerrard and Graeme Revell. Photographed by Dante Spinotti. Edited by William Goldenberg, David Rosenbloom and Paul Rubell. Production Designed by Brian Morris. Special Make-up by Greg Cannom. 157 minutes.

The Coverage: Blindfolded, *60 Minutes* producer Lowell Bergman meets with the leader of a terrorist group about doing an interview with Mike Wallace. The leader agrees, only after Bergman reminds him that *60 Minutes* is the most respected TV news show on the air. The interview is scheduled to take place in two days. Meanwhile, inside his office, Jeffrey Wigand silently packs his belongings and goes home. His wife and children are surprised to find him home so early and at last he confesses that he has been fired. His wife can't believe it. Back in the Middle East, Bergman and *60 Minutes* correspondent Mike Wallace interview the terrorist leader with the same hard-hitting approach they take to everything. Back at his home in Berkeley, Bergman receives a mysterious box of documents that appear to be from inside Philip Morris, one of the largest tobacco companies in the U.S. Bergman calls Doug Oliver, a friend of his, to see if he knows anybody who can help translate the documents. Oliver gives him Wigand's name, but when Bergman calls Wigand, he is unable to even get him on the phone. Bergman tells Wigand that if he wants to meet with him in person, he will be in a hotel lobby in Louisville, Kentucky, where Wigand lives, the next afternoon at 5:00. The next day, as promised, Bergman is there, waiting. When Wigand arrives, they go up to Bergman's room. Bergman shows him the documents and Wigand says that because they are from Philip Morris, he can talk about them. However, he cannot talk about his former employer Brown & Williamson, the number three tobacco company, because he signed a confidentiality agreement. Back at CBS, Bergman finishes editing the segment about the terrorist leader, then directs one of his associate producers to find out everything she can about confidentiality agreements and how to get around them. Back in Louisville, Wigand returns to Brown & Williamson for a meeting with Thomas Sandefur, his former boss. Sandefur tells Wigand that they have a new agreement they want him to sign, and that if he doesn't, his future may be in jeopardy. With his family threatened, Wigand furiously leaves Sandefur's office, refusing to sign the agreement. He calls Bergman and tells him he can't believe that he sold him out. Bergman doesn't know what he's talking about. That night, Wigand visits the driving range alone. But when he spots a mysterious man watching him, he chases him away. The next morning, Bergman arrives at Wigand's house. He has come there to tell him that he never mentioned him to anyone. Wigand is impressed enough by this expression of integrity that he takes Bergman with him and tells him he is scared to say what they were doing at Brown & Williamson. Bergman knows the position Wigand is in: he feels compelled to tell the American people what he knows, but he is afraid of what might happen to him and his family as a result. Bergman tells Wigand that the only person who can decide what to do is him. Back at CBS, Bergman, Wallace and the others try to figure out what Wigand could have to say that is so worrisome to the tobacco companies. Some of the others, however, say they should just forget about it because Big Tobacco has unlimited money and they'll use it to squash anyone who gets in their way. Bergman then wonders about the possibility of forcing Wigand to speak in court. That way, what he says becomes public record and the tobacco companies could do nothing about it. As Bergman explores this possibility, Wigand and his family adjust to life without big money. They are forced to sell their home and Wigand applies for a job teaching high school chemistry and Japanese. Awakened by someone creeping around outside his house, Wigand calls Bergman to tell him he is worried. At last, Bergman and Wigand go to dinner together to discuss the situation. Wigand wonders whether what he is thinking about doing will change anything. Bergman tells him that nothing will be the same once he goes on the air and talks to 30 million people. Wigand remains unsure, but when he receives actual death threats in the form of a vicious e-mail and a bullet in his mailbox, he tells Bergman he wants to do the interview right away, to go on the record before he changes his mind and something happens to him. They can worry about the legal wrangling to get it on the air later. In New York, Wigand and his wife have dinner with Wallace and Bergman. When Bergman brings up the interview, Wigand's wife is shocked – she had no idea he was planning any such thing. Wigand tapes the interview with Wallace, at long last saying what he has waited to say for so long – that the tobacco companies have long known about the addictive power of nicotine and that they have engineered cigarettes in order to enhance delivery of nicotine. This is explosive material, of course, because all the heads of big tobacco, including Wigand's boss, Thomas Sandefur, testified under oath that they did not believe nicotine was addictive. Wallace and Bergman can hardly believe what they are sitting on. Back home, Wigand starts his teaching job. Meanwhile, as a way around Wigand's confidentiality agreement, Bergman has hooked up with Mississippi Attorney General Michael Moore who is suing the tobacco companies for money to pay health-care expenses for sick smokers. The intention is to bring Wigand to court in Mississippi to testify as a witness in their proceeding and thus get his information into the public record. Wigand goes to Mississippi, but is told that a Kentucky court has issued a gag order against him. The gag order has no bearing in Mississippi, but should he testify, he could be arrested and jailed for contempt upon his return to Kentucky. Wigand doesn't know if he can, after all, go through with it. He talks to Bergman and the others, then takes some time to think before returning at last and telling them that he has to do it. He arrives at court and although some tobacco lawyers try to stop him from talking, he testifies anyway. When Wigand arrives back home in Kentucky, he is not arrested, but he is shocked to find that his wife, unable to take the pressure of their situation anymore, has left him and taken their kids with her. Back at CBS headquarters, lawyers explain that they cannot air the story because of a legal concept called 'tortious interference'. Bergman can hardly believe this. Is CBS corporate telling CBS news what they can and cannot do? The worry is that, if convicted of tortious interference, Brown & Williamson could end up owning CBS. Always the investigative journalist, Bergman quickly uncovers what he believes is the real motive behind CBS corporate trying to shut down the story: an FTC filing that shows CBS is being sold to Westinghouse and that the threat of a huge lawsuit from Big Tobacco against the network could jeopardize the sale. CBS news president Eric Kluster says the sale has nothing to do with this, all they want to do is edit an alternate version of the story in which Wigand is neither named nor shown. But Bergman won't have it. When he tries to get support from Wallace, the veteran newsman surprises him by siding with his superiors. In a state of shock, Bergman goes home and tells his wife that he is alone on this one. When Wigand calls, Bergman has no choice but to give him the bad news. Wigand can't believe it. After everything he's been through, he will now only be anonymous? Bergman is as disappointed as Wigand. Returning to his office at CBS, Bergman tells everyone that he will not quit in protest. He will instead stay there and fight to get his story on the air in its original form. But Kluster and Hewitt suddenly produce a 500-page dossier on Wigand detailing a history of dishonesty, violence, emotional problems and run-ins with the law. Hewitt is ready to accept the whole thing and tells Bergman, "You backed the wrong horse." Bergman can't believe it. He calls Wigand and wants to know about all of this. Wigand says it's nothing but Bergman tells him that he's going to have to refute every one of these stories in order to maintain Wigand's credibility. When Bergman finds out that the *Wall Street Journal* is planning to run a story built from the dossier, he hires his own investigators to check out the facts and manages to get the editor to delay the story. Meanwhile, the alternate version of the *60 Minutes* interview – with Wigand's identity hidden – airs that week. Bergman is so upset by this betrayal that he calls a friend of his at the *New York Times* and tells him about what has been going on. The reporter wants to know if Bergman really wants to go through with leaking this story to the press. Bergman is sure. The story runs on page one. Bergman confronts his superiors one last time. He tells them that there is no reason not to run the story in its original form now. Everything that has happened is already out in every other major news outlet. At last, the interview runs with Wigand's name and face unobscured. But it's too late. Bergman quits, telling Wallace, "What got broken here doesn't go back together."

Research: As always, once Mann decided to make *The Insider* (in between the airings of both Wigand interviews on *60 Minutes*) he set to work by engaging in a lengthy pre-production period to research the actual background and events. Much of this research was already present in the form of Marie Brenner's *Vanity Fair* article and in order to go as far as he could with the realistic side of things, Mann decided to have some of the people who participated in the actual events play themselves, such as Mississippi Attorney General Michael Moore. In addition, key scenes around Wigand's decision to testify were recreated where they actually happened. The scene in which Wigand wrestles with the decision to testify takes place in the film exactly where the real event happened and in exactly the same way. The courtroom in which Wigand testifies is the courtroom where that testimony took place. And as he had done on every other film, Mann put his leads through thorough training. So that in addition to meeting their real-life counterparts, Mann even had Crowe conduct chemistry experiments. Not wanting to make a standard docudrama, however, Mann worked hard to uncover the greater meaning behind what was just present in the facts. This greater meaning – "the story of humans in crisis," as he called it – would form the true heart of his story.

Story: In spite of the fact that *The Insider* is based on true events, Mann's basic philosophy remains unchanged. In fact, the truth of the story actually serves to underscore just how true all of Mann's musings about the state of human life are. This has never been some romantic idea or some flight of artistic fancy. This isn't the kind of pop moralism that infects so many candy-coated Hollywood movies. This is real life, and Mann has got the facts to back it up. Everyone in *The Insider* is caught in some kind of deal: Wigand with the tobacco company, Bergman with *60 Minutes*, Wigand with Bergman, CBS News with CBS Corporate, Bergman with the *Wall Street Journal* editor, the *New York Times* reporter, the FBI agent – and the list goes on. For the first time, Mann has brought his philosophy to the level of the everyman. This isn't some criminal like Frank making a deal with a mob boss. Nor is this some supernatural fantasy like the story of Cuza and Molasar. This isn't even just a story of a regular guy caught in some created boundary situation: this really happened. So that even though they are real people, they are nonetheless very full expressions of the Mann Man.

The Mann Man: Both are dedicated professionals. Both compromise themselves in the service of what they mistake for a dream: Wigand took the job with the tobacco company purely for financial gain; Bergman took the job with *60 Minutes* because it gave him clout as a producer. Clearly, Mann is telling us, this is the kind of thing real people do every day. But what sets these men apart is that they both make the hard choice: they give up their deals in order to remain true to what they believe in. Like Murphy in *The Jericho Mile*, Wigand knows that if he doesn't go through with his testimony, he will not be a whole person. And like Cuza in *The Keep*, Bergman must free himself from the corporate monster in order to regain his ideals. These men know they cannot betray themselves or they will be truly lost. Even if it means losing your family, as it really did for Wigand.

Design: Unlike *The Last Of The Mohicans*, Mann didn't stop at executing the film only in a realistic way. He instead managed to overlay the actual realism with design elements that enhance the subtext of the story. This is a film, after all – an artifice. And Mann has never lost sight of the fact that a greater artifice can sometimes lead to a greater truth. Thus, locations serve as spots that become platforms on which something emotional is going to unfold. So, in searching for a spot, Mann looks for places that have a certain feeling or mood. When Wigand is alone in his bedroom and the camera shoots him from the back so that he appears to be going into the corner, that's exactly where he is literally headed. Even details such as a smudge on Wigand's glasses in the scene between him and his wife are purposeful, put there by Mann not only as a reaction against the kind of air-brushed perfection Hollywood so often paints its heroes with, but also to make the audience feel the awkwardness of the man, to get our hearts to go out to him.

Shooting And Cutting: Like *Manhunter*, *The Insider* opens with a remarkable point-of-view shot that is among the most daring and audacious in recent memory. For a full 19 seconds, Mann's camera holds on some image that we cannot identify. Not, that is, until he finally cuts to the reverse angle to reveal Lowell Bergman wearing a blindfold. As with *Heat*, Mann is boldly using a pair of shots as a wordless title and summation of everything that will follow. For what is Bergman at the beginning of the movie but a man in a blindfold being taken for a ride in the service of his job? At the end of the scene, when Bergman finally takes off his own blindfold (what he will metaphorically do as the movie progresses), he finds he has been left alone. In a similar fashion, Mann takes full advantage of the multiple phone calls depicted in the film by deepening the subtext of the scenes through their background. It's no accident that when Wigand calls Bergman about the death threat he's just received, Bergman is in New Orleans standing over a bloody corpse. Or that when Wigand returns home after testifying in Mississippi, they drive past a burning car. For Mann, these are not explicit symbols of something foreboding, but rather a way of raising expectations. In the scene with the burning car, for instance, he concentrated more on the fact that Wigand turns away from the flaming car as if he doesn't want to know what's coming next. What comes next, of course, is that he returns home to find that his wife and family have left him.

Music: After having used some of Lisa Gerrard's music in *Heat*, Mann decided he wanted to employ a significant amount of it in *The Insider*. The overwhelming feeling provided by this music is very religious. These things that these people are going through may appear simple, the music says, but they are in fact life-changing issues so large that they have a spiritual dimension. Ironically, the Gerrard piece that Mann listened to over and over all through pre-production was called 'Sacrifice'.

The Final Word: Mann's greatest achievement to date, *The Insider* earned 7 Oscar nominations, including one for Mann as best director and one for best picture. The film was universally acclaimed for its ability to maintain incredible dramatic tension in spite of the fact that it was little more than one dialogue scene after another. *The Insider*, more than any other Mann film, is supreme testimony to his abilities as a director, a truly towering movie that deserved more than just Oscar nominations. That it lost in all categories to the vapid *American Beauty* is proof positive that Hollywood is more obsessed with rewarding successful ad campaigns and box office totals than real artistic integrity. Position on the Mann Top Ten List: #1.

NB: Both Mann and screenwriter Eric Roth gave up smoking while making this movie. Lowell Bergman and Michael Mann both went to the University of Wisconsin at Madison, but did not know each other at the time. Both Mike Wallace and *60 Minutes* producer Don Hewitt complained about their depiction in the script. Mann chose Christopher Plummer to play Mike Wallace because he had been a fan of the actor since seeing him in the 1969 film *Royal Hunt Of The Sun*. Bergman's line "Are you talking to me or did someone else just walk in here?" is a direct quote of Frank to Leo from *Thief*. Disney chief Michael Eisner was quoted saying he wished he hadn't made *The Insider*.

10. Into The Future Through The Past

Mann's latest production, the controversial Muhammad Ali biopic *Ali* starring Will Smith as 'The Greatest', was one of those on-again, off-again projects that float through Hollywood for years. Originally written by Stephen Rivele and Christopher Wilkinson, the team behind Oliver Stone's *Nixon*, the project had, at various times, other directors such as Barry Sonnenfeld and Spike Lee attached. When Mann stepped in to take over, Spike Lee publicly expressed his anger about Mann being chosen to direct the film because he is white. And the casting of Will Smith, known to most as only the *Fresh Prince Of Bel Air* and one half of the *Men In Black*, had some saying he couldn't cut through his Big Willie style to actually pull off the kind of dramatic turn necessary to bring *Ali* to the screen. But word has it that Ali himself lobbied both for Will Smith and for Michael Mann. Even with Mann attached, the film threatened to be 'off again' when the budget began to cross the $105 million cap Columbia Pictures had set for it. Mann, however, managed to keep the deal in place both by trimming the budget and promising to pay any overages out of his own pocket. The film was released in the US through Columbia Pictures on December 25, 2001.

Ali (2001)

Directed by Michael Mann. Screenplay by Michael Mann and Eric Roth, from a story by Stephen J Rivele and Christopher Wilkinson.

The Cast: Will Smith (Muhammad Ali), Jon Voight (Howard Cosell), Michael Bent ('Sonny' Liston), Jamie Foxx ('Bundini' Brown), Jada Pinkett (Sonji Roi), Paul Rodriguez (Ali's Fight Doctor), Mario Van Peebles (Malcolm X), Mykelti Williamson (Don King)

The Crew: Produced by Michael Mann, A Kitman Ho, Jon Peters and James Lassiter. Music by Lisa Gerrard and Pieter Bourke. Photographed by Emmanuel Lubezki. Edited by William Goldenberg, Lynzee Klingman and Stuart Waks. Production Designed by John Myhre.

The Coverage: Olympic Gold-medallist Cassius Clay surprises everyone when he becomes Heavyweight Champion of the world by defeating 'Sonny' Liston with what would come to be known as the 'phantom punch'. Under the harsh lights of his new-found fame, Clay shocks the world again when, moved by the words of Malcolm X, he joins the Nation of Islam and forsakes his 'slave name' to become Muhammad Ali. Already criticized for his behavior both in and out of the ring, Ali shocks the world again when he refuses to join the Armed Forces and go to Vietnam. He sees no reason why he should fight people who have never oppressed him, especially when there's so much injustice in the US. This divides his fans, making him a hero to some and an object of hate for others. In spite of being offered a deal in which he will only have to serve in the National Guard, Ali refuses to come forward when the draft board calls out "Cassius Clay." Convicted and sentenced to five years in prison, Ali is stripped of his title and forbidden to box. And although he remains free on appeal, his immense wealth is consumed by years of litigation and his questionable financial attachments to the Nation of Islam. Eventually, the Supreme Court reverses his conviction on the grounds of religious freedom. At last allowed to return to the ring, Ali battles his way back, defeating Joe Frazier and George Foreman to regain his Heavyweight Champion title.

Research: As he had with *The Insider*, Mann was interested in telling the 'true' parts of the story as accurately as possible and he worked to enhance that realism in as many ways as he could. When filming the scenes in which Malcolm X preaches to a crowd of young Muslims, Mann referred to a copy of *Malcolm X Speaks*, having underlined key parts of the speeches himself. And while the lead actors in his previous films have had to undergo intense mental or emotional transformations, never before had such an intense physical transformation been required. To prepare for the role, Will Smith alternated between the weight room and the gym with fight trainer Darryl Foster. Working out three hours in the morning and three hours in the evening, the time in between was consumed with studying Ali's speech patterns. As part of the training, which was overseen by Ali's real-life fight trainer, Angelo Dundee, Smith even got the opportunity to spar with such real boxers as former middleweight champion Sugar Ray Leonard. The real Ali visited the gym several times a month to check Smith's progress as he bulked his way toward an incredible 217 pounds. So substantial was the change in Smith's physique that when he ran into Charlize Theron, his co-star from *The Legend Of Bagger Vance*, she couldn't believe her eyes. And if that wasn't enough, because the real Ali loves magic tricks, and visited magic conventions wherever he travelled, magician William Pack was brought in to teach Smith sleight of hand.

Story: Like *The Last Of The Mohicans* and *The Keep*, Mann doesn't just tell us about 'what happened back then' as much as he tells us how important it is to remain true to yourself no matter when you live. *Ali* is not a 'biopic' any more than *The Insider* was a 'docudrama' so that in spite of being based on true events, this is not just the story of a great fighter, but the story of a radical person in radical times, dealing with culture-changing events on a personal level. And unlike *The Insider*, where the events happened largely out of the public eye, the events depicted in *Ali* are world famous, ripped straight from the pages of the history books. In spite of this, however, Mann is not content with mere depiction and is instead intent on filtering it all through the lens of his philosophy so that he can show audiences today how Ali the man exemplifies what Mann holds as the greatest truth.

The Mann Man: As Jeffrey Wigand and Lowell Bergman were before him, so is Muhammad Ali: a real man, yes, but also a Mann Man, completely defined by the moment he is questioned about his conversion to the Nation of Islam. His response is something any one of Mann's protagonists might have said: "I don't have to be the way you want me to be. I'm going to be what I want. And I'm free to think any way I want." It is, in fact, something we could easily imagine Michael Mann himself saying. But while *The Insider* showed us what happens when an Everyman dedicates himself to his beliefs so ferociously, *Ali* shows us what did happen when one of the biggest celebrities of all time did the same. Ironically, in this way, Mann brings his ideas back to the Everyman. It's as if Mann is telling the audience: "If Ali, with all his wealth and influence and power can go through this and come out this way, then so can you and you and you."

Design: Unlike any of his previous films, *Ali* found Mann reaching new levels in his quest for realism. But unlike *The Insider*, where many of the actual locations could be used and many of the actual people involved could simply be brought in, *Ali* presented a challenge in its depiction of events nearly forty years gone. The first task was to assemble a massive library of photographs from Ali's life. These photographs were used extensively for recreating not only such details as furniture styles, but also in defining approaches to lighting and shooting. And when Mann discovered that the famous 5th Street Gym where Ali trained had been demolished, he was able to reconstruct it with complete accuracy thanks largely to this photographic record. In addition to the photographs, all the footage of Ali's fights was also used not merely as a reference for design, but even down to the level of recreating the fights exactly as they occurred, punch for punch. Of course, it also helped that Howard Bingham, Ali's photographer, was present on the set much of the time to act as a sort of eyewitness consultant. Mann's quest for realism was so extensive that when he learned Ali's Miami home circa 1964 still existed, he demanded the location be used for the scenes set there, even though the house now sits directly under the flight path of Miami International Airport and the roaring planes overhead threatened to disrupt the shooting.

Shooting And Cutting: Besides the extensive re-creation of such historic events as Martin Luther King Jr.'s assassination and the Ali fights, one of the biggest challenges facing Mann was how to make the boxing scenes different from what audiences have seen before, especially in the light of such acknowledged classics as Martin Scorsese's *Raging Bull*. To this end, Mann and cameraman Emmanuel Lubezki oversaw the design of a miniature camera set-up, comprised of two lipstick video cameras that transmitted their image to a recorder via a wireless remote belt worn by Mann himself. All told, the set-up was no larger than a cigarette lighter. In this way, Mann was free to dance around the ring with the fighters, moving his tiny camera in wherever he wanted to capture shots that simply would never have been possible without such a rig. The resulting high-definition video footage was then transferred to film and treated by special effects technicians so that it more closely matched the film stock used by the standard motion picture cameras capturing the wider angles. Combined with the fact that Will Smith really took the punches in the ring, the result is exactly what was required by Mann: boxing footage that is not only unsurpassed in its realism, but unlike anything that's ever been seen before.

Music: Following the extensive use of Pieter Bourke and Lisa Gerrard's music in *The Insider*, Mann again returned to them for *Ali*'s underscore. Unlike so many period films, however, Mann didn't want them to do what they called the 'nostalgic signifiers'. In other words, they wanted to bring the '60s alive without falling back on cover versions of '60s songs or styles. Instead, Mann asked for a contemporary flavor with an abstract hint of what Gerrard referred to as "the old coke stoves of Chicago." Recognizing that the film's multiple political and emotional subtexts lifted it above just being a boxing film, Gerrard and Bourke wrote a good deal of music for the film prior to actually seeing any footage. In the end, much of this music met with the approval of their third collaborator: Mann himself. Relying principally on Bourke's percussion and Gerrard's voice, the two composers describe their work as requiring a potency not demanded by their usual songwriting. As with the soundtracks of other Mann films, pre-existing songs are used to comment on the action. And, for the first time, new songs written specifically for the film by contemporary artists (such as R Kelly and Alicia Keys) appear on the soundtrack.

The Final Word: While many film-makers reach their peak somewhere in the middle of their careers, producing their greatest film and then settling back to rest on their laurels and hack their way through the rest of their output as jobbers rather than the artists they (apparently) once were, Michael Mann is not that guy. Judging from his career as a whole, Mann still seems to be seeking out perfection and he only gets better each time he makes another film. If he has proven anything, it is that he is like the men in the stories he tells: dedicated to what he does and adhering to his own personal philosophy no matter the cost. Now all he needs is for the rest of the world to catch up.

11. After Effects

Complete Filmography

Insurrection (1968) Producer, Director

Jaunpuri (1970) Writer, Producer, Director

17 Days Down The Line (1972) Writer, Director

Starsky & Hutch (1975-77; TV) Writer, 'Texas Longhorn' (September 17, 1975), 'Lady Blue' (November 12, 1975), "JoJo" (February 18, 1976), 'The Psychic' (January 15, 1977)

Police Story (1977; TV) Writer

Police Woman (1977; TV) Director, 'The Buttercup Killer' (December 13, 1977)

Vega$ (1978; TV) Writer, 'Pilot' (April 25, 1978)

Straight Time (1978) Writer (uncredited)

The Jericho Mile (March 18, 1979; TV) Co-writer, Director

Swan Song (February 8, 1980; TV) Writer

Thief (1981) Writer, Producer, Director

The Keep (1983) Writer, Producer, Director

Miami Vice (1984; TV) Producer, Co-writer, 'Golden Triangle' with Maurice Hurley (January 18, 1985)

Band of the Hand (1986) Producer

Manhunter (1986) Writer, Producer, Director

Crime Story (1987; TV) Producer, Director, 'Top of the World' (March 6, 1987)

L.A. Takedown (August 27, 1989; TV) Writer, Producer, Director

Drug Wars: The Camarena Story (January 7, 1990; TV) Writer, Producer

Drug Wars: The Cocaine Cartel (January 19, 1992; TV) Producer

The Last Of The Mohicans (1992) Writer, Producer, Director

Heat (1995) Writer, Producer, Director

The Insider (1999) Writer, Producer, Director

Ali (2001) Writer, Producer, Director

As Actor

Kojak (1976), 'By Silence Betrayed' (November 14, 1976) as Dave

Laverne & Shirley (1977), 'Citizen Krane' (April 5, 1977) as Lackey

M*A*S*H (1978), 'Major Topper' (March 27, 1978) as Sergeant Glassberg

Taxi (1978/81), 'Bobby's Acting Career' (October 5, 1978) as Peter Nicholson, 'Zen And The Art of Cab Driving' (March 19, 1981) as Jim's Passenger

Chicago Filmmakers on the Chicago River (1998; documentary) as himself.

Projects Not Realized

Over the course of his career, Mann has been associated with a number of projects. He has said in interviews that the length of time he takes between projects is an irritant, not a choice. But this is only because of his unwavering devotion to making films he truly believes in. Some of the more interesting projects have come about following his success with *The Insider*. Among them is *Gates Of Fire*, based on Steve (*The Legend Of Bagger Vance*) Pressfield's book about the Battle of Thermopylae. This may be Mann's next film, with George Clooney attached as star and co-producer. Leonardo DiCaprio and Mann have tried to work together twice, both times on biopics – one about James Dean, the other about Howard Hughes. He has also been mentioned in conjunction with a biopic about Julius Caesar, to star Tom Hanks. A project called *The Shooter* was to star Brad Pitt. Prior to *The Insider*, Mann was attached to direct *The Zen Differential*, based on William Gibson's cyberpunk novel *Count Zero*. And his follow-up to *Thief* was to be an underworld thriller called *Dark Societies*, using the Far East opium trade as a backdrop.

Books

Ali: The Movie And The Man by Eric Roth (Newmarket Press, December 2001)

Michael Mann's Headgames by Steven Paul Davies, a 54-page book included only with the UK Special Edition DVD of *Manhunter*

Articles

"Making Some Light: An Interview With Michael Mann" by Graham Fuller (*Projections I*, Faber & Faber, 1992)

'The Man Who Knew Too Much' by Marie Brenner (*Vanity Fair*, May 1996; also available online at wwwl.studio.go.com/movies/insider/vanityfair.html)

Websites

Because of his cult status, there are surprisingly few websites devoted to Mann's work as a whole. Instead, sites tend to be devoted to individual films. This list is offered as current at the time of this writing.

http://mannfan.freeservers.com/ – is a Michael Mann fan site that contains some information but has not been updated for a long time.

http://members.spree.com/molasar/ – is a site devoted to *The Keep*. Contains links to seventeen articles about the movie.

http://www.wildhorse.com/MiamiVice/ and http://www.hsanet.net/user/fwilliam/vice/ – are both *Miami Vice* fan sites with extensive FAQs.

http://website.lineone.net/~manhunter/manhunter.html and http://www.manhunter.net/setup.htm – are both *Manhunter* fan sites with lots of pictures and information.

http://www.mohicanpress.com/ – is an incredibly detailed *Last Of The Mohicans* fan site loaded with information.

http://www.geocities.com/Hollywood/Theater/5784/3heat.html – is a *Heat* fan site loaded with sounds and pictures.

The Essential Library: Best-Sellers

Build up your library with new titles every month

Alfred Hitchcock by Paul Duncan, £3.99

More than 20 years after his death, Alfred Hitchcock is still a household name, most people in the Western world have seen at least one of his films, and he popularised the action movie format we see every week on the cinema screen. He was both a great artist and dynamite at the box office. This book examines the genius and enduring popularity of one of the most influential figures in the history of the cinema!

Stanley Kubrick by Paul Duncan, £3.99

Kubrick's work, like all masterpieces, has a timeless quality. His vision is so complete, the detail so meticulous, that you believe you are in a three-dimensional space displayed on a two-dimensional screen. He was commercially successful because he embraced traditional genres like War (*Paths Of Glory, Full Metal Jacket*), Crime (*The Killing*), Science Fiction (*2001*), Horror (*The Shining*) and Love (*Barry Lyndon*). At the same time, he stretched the boundaries of film with controversial themes: underage sex (*Lolita*); ultra violence (*A Clockwork Orange*); and erotica (*Eyes Wide Shut*).

Film Noir by Paul Duncan, £3.99

The laconic private eye, the corrupt cop, the heist that goes wrong, the femme fatale with the rich husband and the dim lover - these are the trademark characters of Film Noir. This book charts the progression of the Noir style as a vehicle for filmmakers who wanted to record the darkness at the heart of American society as it emerged from World War to the Cold War. As well as an introduction explaining the origins of Film Noir, seven films are examined in detail and an exhaustive list of over 500 Films Noirs are listed.

Noir Fiction by Paul Duncan, £3.99

For every light that shines, there must always fall a shadow, a dark side - Noir. Noir has infiltrated our world, like some insidious disease, and we cannot get rid of it. The threads of its growth and development have been hinted at but no-one has yet tried to bind them together, to weave the whole picture. This book takes you down the dark highways of the Noir experience, and examines the history of Noir in literature, art, film, and pulps. Sensitive readers are warned - you may find the Noir world disturbing, terrifying and ultimately pessimistic. Features: Jim Thompson, Cornell Woolrich, David Goodis, James Ellroy, Derek Raymond, Charles Willeford and more.

Woody Allen (Revised & Updated Edition) by Martin Fitzgerald, £3.99

Woody Allen: Neurotic. Jewish. Funny. Inept. Loser. A man with problems. Or so you would think from the characters he plays in his movies. But hold on. Allen has written and directed 30 films. He may be a funny man, but he is also one of the most serious American film-makers of his generation. This revised and updated edition includes *Sweet And Lowdown* and *Small Time Crooks*.

The Essential Library: Recent Releases

Build up your library with new titles every month

Tim Burton by Colin Odell & Michelle Le Blanc, £3.99

Tim Burton makes films about outsiders on the periphery of society. His heroes are psychologically scarred, perpetually naive and childlike, misunderstood or unintentionally disruptive. They upset convential society and morality. Even his villains are rarely without merit - circumstance blurs the divide between moral fortitude and personal action. But most of all, his films have an aura of the fairytale, the fantastical and the magical.

French New Wave by Chris Wiegand, £3.99

The directors of the French New Wave were the original film geeks - a collection of celluloid-crazed cinéphiles with a background in film criticism and a love for American auteurs. Having spent countless hours slumped in Parisian cinémathèques, they armed themselves with handheld cameras, rejected conventions, and successfully moved movies out of the studios and on to the streets at the end of the 1950s.

Borrowing liberally from the varied traditions of film noir, musicals and science fiction, they released a string of innovative and influential pictures, including the classics *Jules Et Jim* and *A Bout De Souffle*. By the mid-1960s, the likes of Jean-Luc Godard, François Truffaut, Claude Chabrol, Louis Malle, Eric Rohmer and Alain Resnais had changed the rules of film-making forever.

Bollywood by Ashok Banker, £3.99

Bombay's prolific Hindi-language film industry is more than just a giant entertainment juggernaut for 1 billion-plus Indians worldwide. It's a part of Indian culture, language, fashion and lifestyle. It's also a great bundle of contradictions and contrasts, like India itself. Thrillers, horror, murder mysteries, courtroom dramas, Hong Kong-style action gunfests, romantic comedies, soap operas, mythological costume dramas... they're all blended with surprising skill into the musical boy-meets-girl formula of Bollywood. This vivid introduction to Bollywood, written by a Bollywood scriptwriter and media commentator, examines 50 major films in entertaining and intimate detail.

Mike Hodges by Mark Adams, £3.99

Features an extensive interview with Mike Hodges. His first film, *Get Carter*, has achieved cult status (recently voted the best British film ever in *Hotdog* magazine) and continues to be the benchmark by which every British crime film is measured. His latest film, *Croupier*, was such a hit in the US that is was re-issued in the UK. His work includes crime drama (*Pulp*), science-fiction (*Flash Gordon* and *The Terminal Man*), comedy (*Morons From Outer Space*) and watchable oddities such as *A Prayer For The Dying* and *Black Rainbow*. Mike Hodges is one of the great maverick British filmmakers.

The Essential Library: Currently Available

Film Directors:

Woody Allen (Revised)	**Tim Burton**	**Ang Lee**
Jane Campion (£2.99)	**John Carpenter**	**Steve Soderbergh**
Jackie Chan	**Joel & Ethan Coen**	**Clint Eastwood**
David Cronenberg	**Terry Gilliam (£2.99)**	**Michael Mann**
Alfred Hitchcock	**Krzysztof Kieslowski (£2.99)**	
Stanley Kubrick	**Sergio Leone**	
David Lynch	**Brian De Palma (£2.99)**	
Sam Peckinpah (£2.99)	**Ridley Scott**	
Orson Welles	**Billy Wilder**	
Steven Spielberg	**Mike Hodges**	

Film Genres:

Film Noir	**Hong Kong Heroic Bloodshed (£2.99)**
Horror Films	**Slasher Movies**
Spaghetti Westerns	**Vampire Films (£2.99)**
Blaxploitation Films	**Bollywood**
French New Wave	

Film Subjects:

Laurel & Hardy	**Marx Brothers**
Steve McQueen (£2.99)	**Marilyn Monroe**
The Oscars®	**Filming On A Microbudget**
Bruce Lee	**Film Music**

TV:

Doctor Who

Literature:

Cyberpunk	**Philip K Dick**	**The Beat Generation**
Agatha Christie	**Noir Fiction (£2.99)**	
Terry Pratchett	**Sherlock Holmes**	
Hitchhiker's Guide	**Alan Moore**	

Ideas:

Conspiracy Theories	**Nietzsche**
Feminism	**Freud & Psychoanalysis**

History:

Alchemy & Alchemists	**The Crusades**
American Civil War	**American Indian Wars**
The Black Death	**Jack The Ripper**
The Rise Of New Labour	**Ancient Greece**

Miscellaneous:

The Madchester Scene	**How To Succeed As A Sports Agent**

Available at all good bookstores or send a cheque (payable to 'Oldcastle Books') to: **Pocket Essentials (Dept MANN), 18 Coleswood Rd, Harpenden, Herts, AL5 1EQ, UK.** £3.99 each unless otherwise stated. For each book add 50p postage & packing in the UK and £1 elsewhere.